EMMA

LEE

JUANITA BROOKS

UTAH STATE UNIVERSITY PRESS

LOGAN, UTAH

Books in the Western Experience Series

Quicksand and Cactus: A Memoir of the Southern Mormon Frontier
Juanita Brooks

John Doyle Lee: Zealot, Pioneer Builder, Scapegoat
Juanita Brooks

Emma Lee
Juanita Brooks

Heaven on Horseback: Revivalist Songs and Verse in the Cowboy Tradition
Austin and Alta Fife

Roping the Wind: A Personal History of Cowboys and the Land
Lyman Hafen

Wild Mustangs
Parley J. Paskett

The Roll Away Saloon: Cowboy Tales of the Arizona Strip
Rowland W. Rider as told to Deirdre Murray Paulsen

Cattle in the Cold Desert
James A. Young and B. Abbott Sparks

Copyright © 1978, 1984
Utah State University Press
Logan UT 84322-7800

10 9   99 00 02 04 06

Library of Congress Cataloging in Publication Data

Brooks, Juanita, 1898-1989
        Emma Lee.

        Includes index.
        1. Lee, Emma, 1836-1897. 2. Mormons—Utah—Biography.
3. Pioneers—Utah—Biography. 4. Utah—Biography.
I. Title
BX8695.L39B76 1984   289.3'32'0924 [B]   84-22057
ISBN 0-87421-121-2 (pbk.)

Contents

Illustrations

Introduction

Juanita Brooks, Unadorned Realist

By Charles S. Peterson

Juanita Brooks was approaching the end of a long and illustrious writing career when she published *Emma Lee* in 1975. Born Juanita Leavitt in 1898 to a pioneering polygamous family at Bunkerville in southern Nevada, she grew up in a Mormon community that was isolated by desert miles as well as by the customs of one of the most distinctive subcultures America has produced. She came to know the lore of her home country as its traditions and geography unfolded through her youthful experiences. Touched now and again by the outside world, she yearned for its broadening influences, but she stayed on to write brilliantly about Mormon Country's Dixie.

Lying mainly in southwestern Utah, but extending into southern Nevada and into the strip of Arizona that lies north of the Grand Canyon, Dixie's early years had been activated by special attention from Brigham Young and given tragic notoriety in the national consciousness by the Mountain Meadows Massacre of 1857. However, the year 1877 had marked the beginning of a quieter, more stable period. That year, change was signaled in an irony of converging events. The dedication of the Mormon Temple at St. George climaxed Brigham Young's determined effort to build the country, and his death vastly diminished the church's special interest in the region's growth, while the execution of John D. Lee, one of the participants at the Mountain Meadows Massacre, at long last quieted national outrage and eased, but did not erase, the local society's sense of guilt and tragedy. For half a century thereafter the country changed but little.

Indeed, if ever the people of Mormon Country had a truly separate existence it was in the Dixie of Juanita Brooks's youth. It lay beyond the railroad, highways had not yet come, "color country" was yet to be discovered. National Parks, movie crews, tourism's hype, sunbelt retirement, and an extension of the garish culture of the Las Vegas Strip were still in the future. With their Mormon sense of community, their isolated but interrelated towns, and their "lore of faith and folly," Dixie's people were as near a self-contained society as could be found in the burgeoning West of the turn-of-the-century decades. Life was limited, opportunities few, and parochialism intense. Self-identity was closely tied to the desert environment. From long experience, people knew the desert's limits and its attributes. Practices and institutions were tailored to its potentials, and in important respects, people belonged to it and shared its character. Even their failed dreams, their secrets, and their moods grew in large measure from their experience in and with the country during the two generations that followed Brigham Young's death.

In this context, the young Juanita grew. From the town of Bunkerville, she absorbed the lore of home. She attended grade school and, by a fortunate turn, was one of the twelve students who made up the first graduating class of Bunkerville's high school. By another fortuitous turn, she also had a year of normal school training there when, as part of a belated effort to upgrade schools, the state of Nevada brought in Mina Connell from Columbia University to teach a one-year course, graduates of which were to receive a temporary teaching certificate. With dreams of education at Columbia implanted in her heart, Juanita Brooks taught a year at neighboring Mesquite and a year at Bunkerville and attended a summer session at the University of Utah. Then followed her short and tragic marriage to Ernest Pulsipher, which ended when he died of cancer in 1921.

Stunned by sorrow and raising an infant son, the young widow found a certain solace in transcribing the pioneer journals of the Pulsipher family, an activity foreshadowing the course of her later life. But to meet immediate needs, she turned to education, first at Dixie College in St. George and then at Brigham Young University, where her interests focused increasingly upon creative writing. On her return to southern Utah, she took a position in 1926 at Dixie College, where she taught English for several years before another "first" influenced her educational life. This time the college offered its first sabbatical leave. Teachers with longer tenure were offered the leave but for reasons of disinterest or family responsibilities turned it down until at last it was offered to her. With no hesitation she accepted. She attended Columbia University, where she received a master's degree in 1929 thus realizing the dream Miss Connell had implanted.

Back in southern Utah, she was appointed dean of women at Dixie College and entered into a life in the community that in 1934 led to her marriage to Will Brooks, county sheriff, who became her chief supporter as she moved into a career as a historian. A federally sponsored project to collect and transcribe the pioneer journals of Mormon Country's Dixie during the depression was her first major step towards history. Later she also wrote articles for *Harper's*, the *Reader's Digest*, and the *Utah Historical Quarterly*. In 1942 a biography of her grandfather Dudley Leavitt became her first book-length publication.

Juanita Brooks's development as a historian during the late 1930s and 1940s was greatly stimulated by a flowering interest in Utah and western topics among a remarkable group of Utah writers, many of whom like herself addressed the past from unlikely freelance backgrounds including literature, journalism, folklore, and sociology. Among the earliest of these to touch her life was Nels Anderson, who became the first writer of what may be called "the Dixie School of Mormon History" when his *Desert Saints*, which approaches the Mormon experience from the standpoint of southern Utah, was published in 1942. Also influential were her uncle LeRoy Hafen and his wife Ann Woodbury, who were already attracting national acclaim for their work in Colorado, mountain man, and Mormon history. Then too the success of *Giant Joshua*, written by her St. George friend Maureen Whipple in the mid-1940s, suggested that Dixie held some interest for publishers. Exerting a somewhat different influence were Utah folklorists Austin and Alta Fife, Hector Lee, and Wayland Hand, who encouraged Brooks to believe that her own roots in the folkways of the region gave her a legitimate claim to the attention of the reading public. During this same period, she formed close and fruitful friendships with historian Dale Morgan and writer Wallace Stegner. She collaborated closely with them in defining the Utah–Mormon topics to which all three turned and helped them identify source materials. Both men read her manuscripts and helped her work out the mix of historical, literary, and folk method by which she addressed the past as well as helped her find publishers and otherwise promoted her career. Less directly involved but still significant were Bernard DeVoto and Fawn Brodie. Encouraged by all these, Brooks was drawn increasingly to the Mountain Meadows Massacre, a study to which she devoted most of the 1940s.

In 1950 *Mountain Meadows Massacre* was published. It immediately gained a widespread recognition and has gone through several printings since. The years that followed saw her bring forth a major publication about every five years as well as take an active role as a board member of the Utah Historical Society. In 1955 came *A Mormon Chronicle: The Diaries of John D. Lee, 1848–1876*, a two-volume work which she edited with California's Robert Glass Cleland. In 1961 her *John Doyle Lee: Zealot—Pioneer Builder—Scapegoat* appeared and in 1964 *On the Mormon Frontier: The Diary of Hosea Stout*, a two-volume work which she edited was published. During the next decade and a half, she published ten additional books, including several family histories; the biography of her husband, *Uncle Will Tells His Story*, and two edited diaries; *Journal of the Southern Indian Mission: Diary of Thomas D. Brown* and *Not by Bread Alone: The Journal of Martha Spence Heywood, 1850 to 1856*. Also belonging to this later period were her autobiography, *Quicksand and Cactus*, which had been written earlier but was published only in 1982, and of course the present book, *Emma Lee*, a biography of one of John D. Lee's wives.

All told, there were fifteen books and scores of articles. With the possible exception of Hosea Stout's *On the Mormon Frontier* and volume one of Lee's *A Mormon Chronicle*, which record midwestern and

Salt Lake Valley phases of Mormon history, Juanita Brooks's works have dealt with Mormon Country's Dixie. These works clearly establish her as the dominant figure in the "Dixie School" and as one of the two or three most distinguished historians of Utah themes.

Perhaps more than any other Utah historian of her time, Brooks emerges as a realist. Like other writers of this persuasion she was attracted to common people and in their doings finds her themes. She is almost narrowly realistic in style and in description of setting, and her treatment of events adheres to a demanding code of honesty. Her characters are plainly and accurately drawn, yet their ultimate worth is never in question. In these qualities as well as in her recognition of the human costs of the frontier experience, she was willing to forego the conventions of romantic and institutional history that prevailed in many quarters during her early years. Indeed, up to her time, Utah and Mormon history had been cast largely in one or more of three stereotypes. For brevity's sake these may be referred to as divine interventionism, devilish subversivism, and romantic nationalism. Each was in its own way institutional history and served the purposes of various established interests.

The premise of most Mormon historians was that the history of the church was essentially the history of God's doings on earth. Since beginning and outcome were fixed and the end glorious, there was a tendency among these historians to regard both the agent and the program as infallible. The human shortcomings of the Saints and the failures of church leaders were glossed over, while the images of both pioneers and churchmen were inflated to verify the truthfulness of the gospel and to provide living models of perfection. Devilish subversivism was the reverse side of this coin and was much used by anti-Mormon writers during the nineteenth century. According to its conventions, Brigham Young was a monster of evil. The Saints were dupes and the Mormon movement a gigantic conspiracy.

With the appearance of Hubert Howe Bancroft's *History of Utah* in 1888, the Mormon experience began to be worked into the literature of romantic nationalism, by which the conquest of the American West was celebrated. Responding in part to nationalism, in part to the West's bigger-than-life landscape, and in part to nostalgic regret at the passing of the West, romantic nationalists, including frontier historian Frederick

Jackson Turner, created heroes—"men to match their mountains"—
as they wrote romantically of conquistadores, mountain men, explorers,
railroaders, cowboys, miners, and pioneers. As intellectual historian
Vernon Parrington explained in an introduction to a reprint of O. E.
Rölvaag's *Giants in the Earth*, romantic nationalism put the history of
the West in a

> broad and generous perspective . . . [that] responded most sympathe-
> tically to the epic note that runs through the tale of the conquest of the
> continent. It is the great American romance that gives life and drama
> to our history . . . the poetry of America in the silent march of a race
> toward the far-off Pacific, hewing its way triumphantly through forests
> and mountains to arrive at its objectives.

In the hands of the romantic nationalists, the Mormon story had
become part of a larger mosaic, an element in a grand national adventure, which, if not actually orchestrated by Providence, represented
some sort of great and inevitable continental dynamic. For the larger
national story to be effective, it became necessary for the Mormon story
to be a success. And so it was couched. Brigham Young was master
colonizer, a man fit for the grandest mountains. Mormon pioneers were
heroic figures redeeming desert wastes in elemental confrontation. In
this interpretation, the Mormon story supported the national interest as
surely as the institutional history of Mormondom supported the church
and ultimately differed little from it.

Juanita Brooks rejected these three approaches to the past. In
Mountain Meadows Massacre and her other Dixie works she substituted
the realism of the commonplace and an affinity for the unadorned truth.
Her writing reveals no wish to adopt values of other cultures nor any
secret hankering for New York, Cambridge, or even the Huntington
Library in California, with which she was associated for a time in the
1940s. To the contrary, she accepted what she was with finality. First,
last, and always she was practical and down-to-earth—a product of the
folk culture of Mormon Country's Dixie in its most isolated period.
She wrote always with determination to not let historical conventions
or intellectual abstractions distort or limit the events she described.
Her approach to the past sprang, in the final analysis, from a sincere
love of truth, a native loyalty to her own locality, and a deep conviction

that the human spirit is a noble thing that will eventually endure against all odds.

Fundamentally, Brooks's affinity for her own people reflects a sense for the underdog that is itself an extension of her person and the experience of her life. From the beginning, she came in every back door there was to enter. She was a scrawny, disadvantaged child in the blistered desolation of southern Nevada, suffered more than her share of setbacks in her youth and local schooling, met immediate tragedy in her first marriage, faced the disadvantages of being a woman and a "country hick" in the higher education system. She was employed outside her discipline at an unknown college, and she picked up a forgotten function of history and breathed life into an entire state in her Public Works Collection tasks of the 1930s. Later she was determined to write about forbidden topics and scapegoats and found it necessary to go underground, virtually leaving only back doors open to her. It is little wonder that she, an underdog herself, wrote about the Mountain Meadows Massacre and John D. and Emma Lee.

As Brooks's book about Emma Lee suggests, women featured largely in her historical interests. This is particularly true of women who for one reason or other lived at what she might have called "the ragged edge." Her approach to women carried some awareness of their role as underdogs but otherwise was unadorned—practical and down-to-earth. She learned about them at quilting bees, in kitchen and parlor conversation, from pioneer journals and letters, and, of course, from personal experience. Although many of the women about whom she wrote were her relatives, she resisted the limitations implicit in the adoring tones and sunbonnet stereotypes used by many of her contemporaries as she had resisted romantic conventions that cast masculine pioneers in heroic dimensions. For one thing, many aspects of pioneering persisted in Dixie until well into Juanita Brooks's life. Pioneer functions were commonplace activities not yet surrounded by romance and reverence. Her women came through as mothers (both loving and overbearing), entertainers, promoters of culture, educators, midwives, business managers, and as having real force in the society. She took them seriously, yet approached them with an eye to color and drama with a folksy sense of humor that kept sacrifice, monotony and achievement, as well as pride, in perspective.

Her concern for the woman's part allowed her to see into matters of Indian relations with particular perception. Indeed, the very best article ever written on the history of Utah's Indian women is her piece of almost monographic length that appeared in the 1944 *Utah Historical Quarterly*. In it, she described the immediate and long-term impacts of an 1852 law allowing for the indenturing of Indian children. Under its terms, many Indian children were taken into white homes. While most died, enough survived to provide a rich local lore. Most of those who remained in the white community were female. Some married white men. Others did not. Quite a number bore children and raised families. All lived between two worlds but for the most part did it with dignity and courage. By the time Brooks approached the subject, the descendants of these women had been integrated into the white community and retained little or no connection with Indians of the area.

Although this article preceded the development of ethnohistory by several decades, its attention to detail and folkways foreshadowed in important respects an entire genre of Indian studies that developed in the 1970s. Here again her writing is devoid of romantic eulogistic elements. Drawing from local and oral sources as well as from government documents, she portrays Indian women under the impact of conquest with fidelity and quiet compassion, rare among white writers.

And of course there was Emma Lee. Here was the underdog par excellence—Juanita Brooks's own kind of person, one about whose back doors and tragedies her own back doors and tragedies had prepared her to write. Coming to Utah with the Martin and Willie Handcart Companies, Emma Batchelor Lee cut into the most tragic event of Mormon migration, knew the worst and the best of polygamy, and came as near the starkest tragedy of the West's entire history as one could without either being killed or killing someone else at Mountain Meadows. The melancholy recesses of Lonely Dell, the second marriage to a drifting prospector, and her last years in the barren windswept railroad town of Winslow, Arizona, continued the theme for Emma Lee. They were indeed back doors to an early and estranged death. Brooks rescues Emma Lee from obscurity, brings her out of the wilderness, and demonstrates that the human spirit often rises to real dignity even in the most unpromising circumstances. Emma Lee's story is its own kind of success story—one that Brooks knew well because she had lived many of the elements herself.

In her biography of Emma Lee, Brooks wrote in what Wallace Stegner termed "the broad borderlands of history" in a 1965 *American West* article. Documentary evidence was thin, so Brooks not only wrote historically but lapsed into fiction as she provided dialogue to help tell the story and drew from regional tradition and family lore to flesh out the account. Stegner, who employs similar methods, defends such liberties. In his biography of IWW martyr, Joe Hill (*The Preacher and the Slave*), Stegner went beyond documentation, filling out both the setting and the narrative to provide a context in which the dramatic events of Joe Hill's known history could find proper impact. Collecting documentary evidence and "walking through a mock execution so that I could know imaginatively how a condemned and blindfolded man might feel," Stegner came to know IWW history as well as anyone in the world. Similarly, in *Wolf Willow* Stegner, who had "grown up literally without history, in a place where human actions had not been formally remembered," fashioned a past for the Cypress Hills area of southern Saskatchewan. In the process, he drew about a third of his information from reminiscence, a third from history, and another third from his imagination. As he explained, "I thought I could get more truth into a slightly fictionalized story." Dale Morgan often admonished Brooks to abandon a tendency to mix history and fiction in her writing; and in the *Mountain Meadows Massacre* and other books and edited works of the 1950s and 1960s, she hewed to carefully disciplined and closely defined history. But in her later life, she returned to the "borderlands" of history once more. She knew the history of southern Utah, including the Mountain Meadows Massacre, better than anyone. She had also walked with Emma Lee far beyond the limits of the recorded past and knew her feelings and her aspirations. Thus with realistic honesty, she has created for Emma Lee a past that fits her role in western history.

Like Brooks's other writings, *Emma Lee* reveals much about the workings of place in her own life and in the lives of the people about whom she writes. From experiences unfolding from birth, she developed a keen sense of place and of the interdependencies between herself, her community, and the environment. While she knew intuitively the country's limits and understood that bounds within it as well as around it changed and varied with time, there was an eminently practical quality in her approach to place. Place was something you lived in and with which you coped. You took its measure and found it to be manageable. Its austerity could be adjusted to, its heat, winds, dust, and distances borne. Its threat as well as its beauty and grandeur were so much in surfeit, so near at hand, and so mixed with monotony and boredom that emotional response was subordinated to the matter-of-fact and the realistic. With Juanita Brooks even love of place and sense of its appropriateness were true-life forms, limited in dimension and importance by her remarkable penchant for seeing things as they were. As a result, one searches in vain in her writing for the grandiloquent and mystical language with which so many western writers have responded to the romance of western landscapes. She was, after all, too close to it; too distant from the promotional and romantic impulses that teach us to rhapsodize about the beauties of the West to understand that any less practical view was possible.

Nevertheless, her sense of place did go beyond the practical to the intuitive — to moods and to innuendoes that were no less real because they belonged in the realm of feeling rather than to the empirical. Understanding her attachment to specific places within the larger context of Dixie may help explain this. With respect to moods of well being, of intimacy, of order and belonging, and of adaptation to desert rhythms, Bunkerville and St. George best symbolize her thrust. In the terms of anguish, of failed dreams, and of tragedy there can be no doubt that Mountain Meadows was central. With its topography and plant life transformed by overgrazing from the verdure of high-country meadow to the harshness of eroded sagebrush plateau, even its very biological presence seemed a reminder of failed dreams and tragedy. From it emanated a complex of tragic feelings that touched the lives of the entire society and for decades placed a limiting and distorting hand on that society's perception of its past. As Brooks well knew, place and event had worked together to give the region a unique identity and to provide a special texture to its culture. If any locality in the history of western Mormondom can approach the importance of Salt Lake City in either regional or national awareness, it is Dixie. This is so precisely and specifically because of the events that occurred at Mountain Meadows and because of the way memory and mood have worked to join people and place.

Finally, one sees in *Emma Lee* a strain of melancholy that lends a special resonance to Juanita Brooks's sense of place. Less central than the tragic mood, melancholy comes to focus on the person of Emma Lee, a hapless bystander, caught and drawn into circumstances not of her making. Place as associated with Emma Lee has a particularly melancholy quality. At New Harmony, at the oasis points beyond the Colorado River, at Winslow, and most indelibly at Lonely Dell, it is a hovering presence. From these places yearning, frustration, sorrow, fear, and loneliness cast lingering shadows. But ultimately there was in the relationship of Emma Lee and place the practical quality of coping and surviving that so characterizes Juanita Brooks's perception of reality. A product in part of her place, Emma Lee is plainly and honestly portrayed, but because there is no alternative persists against overwhelming odds.

Those who read this new edition of *Emma Lee* will share in an appreciation for Juanita Brooks's understanding that moods lend both form and dimension to the texture of local experience. They will also realize that she saw beyond tragedy and melancholy to the basic goodness of the human spirit and will stand to profit from her recognition of the roles women played in the most dramatic events of western history.

Emma Batchelor

of England

The carving on her headstone says that Emma Batchelor was born in Uckfield, Sussex County, England, April 21, 1836, and died November 16, 1897. From family records we learn that she was the daughter of Henry and Elizabeth Divel Batchelor and had a sister, Frances, and a brother, Henry, and very probably another sister who remained in England.

Of her early life we know little, but her writing gives evidence of a good education, while her skill in all the household arts and her immaculate cleanliness show careful training in the home. Strong-willed, she was sometimes sharp and positive in expressing her opinions. On the other hand, she was very tenderhearted and gentle, especially with anyone injured.

For the long period beginning in the 1830s, England was struggling with problems of overpopulation, unemployment, and poverty. The Queen was encouraging settlement in Canada, Australia, and other areas where there was space and opportunity, so that when the Mormon missionaries arrived in England they found a field literally "ripe unto the harvest." Their new gospel was not just an appeal to prepare for the second advent; it held out hope of free land, with a chosen people already gathering.

Best of all, ways were provided by which converts might go to Zion with a minimum of expenditure. Chartered ships would carry them across the ocean; a railroad would take them from the coast to the heart of the continent—the Mississippi River. From there they could walk the remainder of the way, pulling their belongings on a handcart furnished by the Church, while supply wagons attending the train would ration out their food. It sounded so simple, so easy! One mode of payment was to sign on the dotted line contracting to give one-year's labor to the Church in whatever way they could best serve.

Enthusiasm ran high. Over a period of three or four years, thousands were converted and waited their turn to come. They sang the songs of Zion, among them "The Handcart Song": "For some must push, and some must pull, as we go marching up the hill! So merrily on our way we go, until we reach the Valley, O!"

Two of the most eager of all the converts were Emma Batchelor and her friend Elizabeth Summers. They made their plans together, selected their clothing, and later, they shared the necessary cooking utensils and supplies. The record lists Emma as twenty-one years of age, Elizabeth as twenty-seven. They were passengers on the last ship to leave Liverpool that season, the *Horizon*. This ship, under the leadership of Captain Edward Martin, was carrying 856 Utah-bound passengers, and did not sail from port until May 25. Though they had a good voyage and adequate train connections after the landing, the passengers did not reach Iowa City until July 8.

Here they found the James G. Willie Company, which had sailed three weeks ahead of them, still waiting for their handcarts. Brother Levi Savage, looking over this crowd of more than 1,000—among them many elderly, many children, a sprinkling of pregnant women—felt they should stop in Iowa City and set up winter quarters. Here it was the middle of July; the journey to Zion required 100 days under normal conditions. Some teams traveled it in three months but such companies could be over the mountains before winter set in. Under the best of conditions, the Martin and Willie companies could not make it—not even those who got on the road first.

The Saints were eager to reach their destination, of course; most of the Elders voted to go on. Only Brother Savage spoke out firmly against proceeding.

"Brothers and Sisters: What I have said, I know to be true; but seeing that you are determined to go forward, I will go with you, will help you all I can, will work with you, rest with you, will suffer with you, and, if necessary, I will die with you. May God in His mercy bless and preserve us."

Emma and Elizabeth had been among those who shouted:

"On to Zion! God will temper the wind to the shorn lamb! On to Zion! O ye of little faith!" Later Emma had plenty of time to regret this and in remorse doubled her efforts to help her companions.

Since the Willie Company was not as large as the Martin Company, a few were permitted to transfer into it as the handcarts were finished. Emma and Elizabeth were among those transferred. By the time the carts had been a few weeks on the road, they began to show wear; many had to be repaired. By the time the Willie Company reached Fort Laramie, the Captain ordered all members to lighten their loads. Specifically, Sister Emma was ordered to leave behind a brass kettle in which she was carrying her belongings. This she refused outright to do. Instead she set it by the side of the road, and remained sitting on it, while Elizabeth doubled with a family whose cart was broken down and went on.

Emma knew that the Martin Company was only about ten days behind, so she sought shelter at the fort and did laundry and mending for the commander's wife to pay for her food and bed. When the Martin Company came up, she joined her friends and neighbors, the Paul Gourley family.

"Here we were joined by Sister Emma Batchelor," wrote the young son years later. "We were glad to have her, because she was young and strong, and it meant more flour for our mess."

At Fort Laramie Sister Gourley gave birth to a child; Emma acted as midwife and afterward helped pull the mother on the cart for two days. Emma also carried young Paul over the streams to keep his feet dry.

We cannot detail the horrors of this trip, when the storms came early and death stalked everywhere, when the ground was so frozen tent pegs could not be driven into it, when the dead could not be buried. No definite figure has ever been published of the number of deaths in the Martin Company; an estimate, probably too low, sets it at 150.

Almost as tragic as the deaths were those left maimed for life with frozen feet, ears, noses, or fingers. Though the casualties in the Willie

Company were less than half those in the Martin Company, Emma's friend Elizabeth was one who lost most of her toes.

A year later, when Emma was introduced to Brigham Young and he was surprised that she had come through the ordeal whole, she told him:

"Brother Brigham, I had no one to care for me or to look out for me, so I decided that I must look out for myself. I was one who called out to go when Brother Savage warned us. I was at fault in that, but I tried to make up for it. I pulled my full share at the cart every day. When we came to a stream, I stopped and took off my shoes and stockings and outer skirt and put them on top of the cart. Then, after I got the cart across, I came back and carried little Paul over on my back. Then I sat down and scrubbed my feet hard with my woolen neckerchief and put on dry shoes and stockings."

On their arrival in the valley, people were taken into different homes to recover from the effects of the journey. Emma was placed in the home of a Brother Kippen, where she worked as a servant to his wife. The paper she signed promised that she would serve one year, and the implication was that after the year she would become his plural wife. Emma did not see it that way at all. She did not like the woman who treated her as a servant and ordered her about and criticized her; she had less than admiration for her husband, repulsing firmly every advance he made. So at the end of the year, she sought employment elsewhere.

She was ready to get married, but as yet she had not seen a man who appealed to her. Sooner or later he would come, she told herself.

Courtship and Marriage

It was Sunday, December 27, 1857, and Emma was attending the afternoon meeting in the Thirteenth Ward. Bishop Edwin D. Woolley was presiding. From early times, this ward had been noted for its good choir and for its excellent services, so that out-of-town visitors often attended here.

Bishop Woolley came forward to call the meeting to order.

"Brothers and Sisters," he said. "It is time to begin our meeting. The opening prayer will be offered by Brother John D. Lee, who is here attending the legislature from Washington County. Brother Lee."

Emma was instantly impressed. She liked his voice; she liked the way he turned his sentences, she liked his looks in general. Here now was a man a girl could look up to.

Lee's diary says only, "We had quite [a] good Meeting." Early in the meeting, Lee became conscious of an attractive young lady facing him in the audience about four rows back. Their eyes met. Emma smiled and dropped her eyes and toyed with her handkerchief. He never caught her glance again, though he knew that she knew he was trying to get her attention.

Years later as Emma's teenage son waited with her to give birth to her last child, he said, "I think Father should be here." Emma spoke sharply, "He would be here if he could get here," she told him. "Your father is a man of God. I knew it the instant I heard him speak. I loved him from the minute I saw him and would have married him right then, if he'd asked me. And I've never been sorry—not once—that I am his wife."

She might say this years later, but on that Sunday in 1857, Emma quickly lost herself in the crowd. She did not know that Brother Rollins (with whom Emma was staying) and John D. Lee had crossed the plains in the same company; she didn't know that Rollins had invited Lee to dinner after the meeting.

When John and Emma were introduced, he told her that she was even more attractive in her white apron and later that her biscuits were like none he had ever tasted before, and the roast had new and teasing flavor also. And did she have a partner for the dance tomorrow night? Would she care to go with him?

So they went on their first date in a fancy buggy drawn by a fine team, all borrowed from Brother Judson Stoddard. How Brother Lee could dance! He acted as if he really enjoyed the quadrilles and polkas, some of which Emma had never tried. As they drove home and he tucked the robe about her, he asked, "Happy?" After a pause she answered, "Very."

Instead of taking Emma back to Brother Rollins's house for the night, John took her to the home of his oldest daughter, Sarah Jane Dalton. It was closer; he could put up the horses there, feed them, and have them to use the next day.

Sarah Jane was about Emma's age, and they liked each other at once. After breakfast and the morning duties, Lee took them to town. He let them each select a pretty "fascinator," a fine shawl to cover the head, and a fancy handkerchief. Sarah Jane and Emma had their pictures taken together. John had his taken alone, in his tall silk hat.

They visited several stores, and ate cookies and ice cream. They passed the Salt Lake Theater, and Lee made a date to go to the play next Friday.

Sarah Jane was taken back home in the early afternoon to allow John and Emma time for getting acquainted by themselves. Emma did not record their conversation, but John entered in his diary: "Emma expressed an attachment for me & Said that I on first site was the object of her Choice." He went on to tell her he would consult Brother Brigham about it and let her know his decision.

"Why not do it right now?" Emma said. "If he has time, it will be better to talk it out now, and if he wants to put it off a while, well, we can appoint the time."

Lee, flattered by her willingness and forthright readiness to meet the President, left her sitting in the buggy while he went alone to see if this would be a good time to present Sister Batchelor. And John was pleased at Emma's composure. She acted as though talking to the Prophet was an everyday occurrence. Brother Brigham listened to her story of the handcart experiences and her reaction to the first man into whose home she was sent, and he seemed impressed. He told her to make preparations and come next Thursday morning, when he would perform the ceremony.

At noon, January 7, 1858, President Brigham Young pronounced John D. Lee and Emma Batchelor husband and wife, united for time and eternity. This was done in his own private Sealing Room, with a few members of the legislature and Lee's daughter Sarah Jane Dalton as witnesses. Ezra T. Benson ran a boarding house for the traveling public and for members of the legislature who came from distant parts of the territory. Having heard of the wedding, Sister Benson baked and decorated a beautiful cake, while Lee provided drinks for the crowd, and they had a celebration.

In the meantime, Bishop Isaac C. Haight of Cedar City had married Emma's friend Elizabeth Summers. At the close of the legislature, the two couples started south in the same large wagon, heavily loaded. Emma and Elizabeth had plenty to talk about since that day when Emma so stubbornly sat on her brass kettle and watched the company go on without her. Still, she felt that God's hand had truly been over her—the help she had been able to give to the Gourley family had saved the life of the mother, and little Paul was probably spared his feet. After all, it seemed that things would work out for the best.

A strange honeymoon trip this, in a wagon, in the dead of winter. But they did not have to camp out at all; each night they spent in a home with a warm evening meal and a comfortable bed. In regular trips over this road the pattern had been set: they paid for their accommodations and the feed for their animals. Lee's diary lists each stop from the day they left Salt Lake City on Monday, January 25, 1858, to their arrival at the fort at Harmony. For Emma this trip had been a true honeymoon; John D. had also become convinced that this wife would stand by him.

Emma proved her commitment to him. It was only a trifling thing, but to Lee it seemed significant. At Beaver they had picked up the two Woolsey boys, nephews of his wives Aggatha and Rachel. As they were already overloaded, the team began to fail. At noon they were overtaken by Richard Benson, driving a fresh team on a new wagon. He stopped and invited them to ride with him to Parowan. They would get there earlier and all would ride more comfortably. Isaac and Elizabeth accepted his offer gladly, as did the two Woolsey boys, who took their bedrolls and sacks with them also.

They urged Emma to come along, too; she would get in out of the cold, they said. But Emma preferred to stay along with her husband; this wasn't cold at all, she told them. "No, thank you very much, but I am very happy right here," she insisted. The night was cold but Emma was warm in her new marriage. For this moment she had endured the handcart experience. She did not know then that John's involvement in the Mountain Meadows Massacre just a few months before would haunt their life together for twenty years, bringing hardship, pain, and tragedy. For now, the future seemed bright; she was Emma Batchelor Lee, a young bride on her way to her new home.

Lee was so impressed that he wrote in his diary for that day: "(Reflections) Emma is the 1st English girl that [has been] Given me in the covenant of the P.H., & a more kindhearted, industrious, & affectionate wife I never had. She covenanted to follow me through Poverty, privation, or affliction to the end of her days & I believe that her intntions real & integrity true."[1]

At Parowan, they all had dinner with President William H. Dame, and both he and Bishop Haight spoke at a night meeting, especially called because they were in town. After having spent two weeks in Great Salt Lake attending the legislature and being in the company of President Brigham Young every day, they should have plenty to report to the people of Parowan.

As they left town the next morning, Lee's wagon broke through the ice at Coal Creek, and in the struggle to get it out, the tongue was broken, which delayed them almost another day.

"About nine o'clock at Night I reached home," he wrote in his diary on Friday, February 5, 1858. "Myself & Emma was kindly recieved with a cordial welcome by my Family. . . ."

Emma Lee of Harmony

Emma knew in general the extent of John D. Lee's family—the early wives, Aggatha and Rachel Woolsey, sisters; Lavina and Polly Young, also sisters; and Sarah Caroline Williams—all of whom were with him before the move west. Of other wives who deserted after they

---

[1]*Editorial Note:* John D. Lee's diaries are noted for their vivid detail and provide important information about Emma Lee. However, as Brooks has mentioned elsewhere, "Lee's spelling like much of the spelling of the western frontier at that time, showed little respect for the authority of Noah Webster." See *A Mormon Chronicle: The Diaries of John D. Lee, 1848-1876*, edited and annotated by Robert Glass Cleland and Juanita Brooks, 2 vols. (San Marino, California: The Huntington Library, 1955).

left Nauvoo, she knew nothing, nor needed to know, for living conditions were hard. A husband absent for months on trips for food and supplies, then gone again on a long trek to Santa Fe to secure money from the Mormon Battalion, might expect beautiful young girls to find other companions.

Martha Berry and Mary Leah Groves had been married to John D. Lee after they all arrived in Zion, but Martha had left him to marry another man, her two living daughters choosing to live with their Grandmother Berry and her only son, Orson, remaining with his father. Mary Leah Groves spent a great deal of time with her parents, and at last made her home with them, as they needed her help. Then there was the girl-wife, Mary Ann Williams, who had been "sealed" to Lee when she was only fourteen with the understanding that she should not become his wife in fact until after she was eighteen unless she herself desired it. Emma and Mary Ann would share the room left vacant by Martha Berry.

Emma at once entered into the business of cooking and kitchen work, for this was her specialty. She took hold with a cheerful efficiency, which they all appreciated. Not until breakfast was over and the kitchen in order did she venture outside. She and Mary Ann had shared the dishwashing and together they went out to look over the area in general.

The double gates of the fort were on the north, and straight through across from them was the Meeting House; the Lee family quarters were all on the west side; the well was in the center of the fort; and the outhouses were outside the enclosure. Across the road were the stockyards and corrals, all picketed in by upright cedar posts, and the farmland stretched far to the north and east in a great expanse.

Would she and Mary Ann like to get into the wagon and ride up to where the new Big House was being built? Would they! John Alma, Lee's oldest son, had the outfit ready. His father had been called to a meeting with some of the other brethren; the women were all busy with their own affairs, so the three of them would go. Emma quickly sensed the relationship between Mary Ann and John Alma. They were in love!

This trip was a revelation to her—the spreading expanse of land, with several men plowing and others cleaning out ditches. Two men were plastering Mary Leah Grove's apartment in the fort; Emma had noticed several references to Mary Leah's strong home ties. On they went, past the two-story "Mansion House" to be shared by Aggatha and Rachel. Here workers were putting on the roof. They continued up to a spot near the Lone Pine, where Alma turned the buggy around.

"Oh, what a scene! What a scene!" Emma cried. "I'd like my place to be high up here, where there is a running stream and trees and this view."

She felt a certain pride in belonging to this great undertaking, with so many employed and such an air of accomplishment everywhere.

On Monday, February 8, 1858, Lee went south with Brother Joseph Horne to select an area for the experimental cotton farm that was about to be established. For several days they evaluated sites, considered places for dams where the water could be taken out for irrigation, and determined the quality of the soil. Having been raised in the South, Lee was much interested in the new settlement to be called Washington. He purchased a lot and sixteen acres for which he paid Mr. Hawley $150.00 in cattle. "My intention is to raise Cotton," he wrote.

He returned to spend the week roofing the "mansion" at Harmony. Aggatha and Rachel would occupy this house, where the family hall would be large enough for parties and sociables.

The snow during the next weeks would mean water and moisture for next year, but Lee used it as another reason to go back to his place in Washington. Here, by March 23, it was spring. His young fruit trees, grape vines, and garden seed should all be planted quickly. So taking his wife Polly Young, and Terressa Morse Chamberlain (later to become Lee's wife), his son Alma, and an Indian boy, Lem, he set out. He also took two "milch" cows along, as necessary to any family.

He at once selected three lots which were yet unclaimed and proceeded to mark them off, set up the boundaries, and enclose them in a brush fence. These might prove useful, he reasoned.

During this time, there was a call for teams and wagons to move Salt Lake City's inhabitants south if the impending "Utah War" made flight necessary again. As always, Lee fitted up more than anyone else. He also donated a beef for the teamsters.

For Emma, this was interesting but unimportant. Lee was glad when she persuaded Elizabeth Haight to come and spend a few days with her, while their husbands were both away.

But now it was time for everyone to be busy, for "no seeds planted, no harvest."

In early May, Emma worked with two of the other wives to help get the crops planted. A week later, she was again ready to help John D., this time in Washington. He wanted to plant cotton, and he took a wagon, four horses, his oldest son and Mary Ann. John D. didn't guess how wonderful this was for the two young people to have some time together. But Emma knew. On June 3 the party returned to Harmony with everyone helping to pick a bushel of berries on the way.

So the spring passed. And Emma was busier still because John D. planned to celebrate the Fourth of July inviting all the Saints in the southern part of the state.

This would take a great deal of preparation. On June 29, 1858, he built a kiln to dry malt for the beer. He had six bushels of his own wheat malted and others donated enough to make 300 gallons of good malt beer. "I also was busily engaged with 12 hands Painting, Papering, & fitting up My Mansion to recieve the company, consisting of the Priesthood, Brass Band, choir, &c of this stake of Zion, Numbering between 4 & 500 Persons besides the citizens of this Place."

Certainly the little village of Harmony never had so impressive a celebration either before this event or after. John D. Lee fed between 400 and 500 people, using some 2,000 pounds of meat, together with vegetables of all kinds, pies, cakes, and malt beer. Filling the forenoon was a parade, numbers by the band and choir, an oration by E. Morris of Cedar City, toasts, and sentimental speeches.

The dinner was served from 1 to 4 p.m. after which dancing began. The company stayed overnight—sixty couples occupying his upper hall, and the others finding beds in their vehicles or on the grass or the haystacks.

John D.'s son John Alma had been sent as an interpreter to the White Mountain Mission, which left Mary Ann more free to help Emma in the kitchen, though John D. thought nothing of that.

During this season, Lee continued to buy land in Washington. In September, he was busy cutting up his corn crop there and working his cane into molasses. He had bought a farm of about thirty acres and also three city lots from people who wanted to move away. He also planned to establish a tannery there for the preparing of leather.

During the late fall of 1858, teamsters from the East began passing through to California. Many had come with the army; others were gold seekers who chose the southern route. Lee had a large sign of an eagle placed over his door, and for a few weeks his house was full every night.

In fact one night, seventy-six people put up at the Lee "mansion," and the family never went to bed, staying up to cook and wait on the travelers. Emma and three of her sister wives were exhausted by cooking for such a crew, but with thirty-one cents per meal, the money was welcome.

But more important than anything else was the marriage of John D.'s son John Alma to Mary Ann Williams. It would seem that earlier in the season, John D. had attempted to make love to Mary Ann and to claim his rights as her legal husband. Even though she was sealed to him in the New and Everlasting Covenant, she would not honor this agreement.

> I told her that if [I] could not make her happy that she should have her liberty, and if there was any other man that she could be more hapy with, to say so & I would use my endeavors to have her seald to that man. She replied that she could love me and respect me as a Father but not as a husband, and that she wantd my oldest son for her companion & that she loved him more than any other Man that She ever saw. Upon reflection I answered that her request Should be grantd. Under those considerations I Married them at the time above specified [January 18, 1859], and I gave them a sumptious Supper and Social Party in my Family Hall to which I invited all the inhabitants of Harmony. . . .

How pleased everyone was, especially Emma, who all along had known the situation and hoped for this.

By February, Lee had almost finished the fine stone mansion in Washington, and was building a stone fence in front of it "2 feet wide at bottom & one at top. Stone dressed & neatly laid up in Mortar . . . ."

By March 15 he had the house shingled. Now he would have a "mansion" in Washington more impressive than the one in Harmony. Here the two Young sisters, Polly and Lavina, would live. When the factory was finished, they would all be employed there.

If Emma rejoiced at the happiness of Mary Ann and John Alma, she might well have been shaken a bit by John D.'s next marriage, to Terressa Morse Chamberlain, even though Brigham Young had sanctioned it and Amasa M. Lyman was there to perform the ceremony, on March 18, 1859. As background we know little: Terressa Morse had married Solomon Chamberlain, who was thirty-two years older than she and whose disposition did not improve with the years, as hers also did not either. Lee spoke of her eldest son, Charley, sometimes as Charley Wilson, sometimes Charley Chamberlain, and sometimes just "good old Charley." Charley came into the Lee home with his mother.

Her second son, Robert, was just one year younger than Charley, but he remained with his father. The daughter, Louisa, lived with her father also, though she was only ten years old; and after two years she went to work in the household of Lemuel H. Redd and later became his plural wife.

The Chamberlain family had come south in John D. Lee's company of nineteen wagons, which arrived at Parowan on November 4, 1851, and went on with him to establish Harmony in 1852. Later Brother Chamberlain moved on south to join the settlers in Washington, where he died March 20, 1862.

For a time Emma had to share her quarters with Terressa, but she resolved not to be jealous of anyone. Her concern was to keep a place in her husband's heart that would be all her own by putting his welfare before everything else, by serving meals that he could be proud of, and by maintaining a haven to which he could come whenever he was weary or discouraged.

She was skilled in all the household arts; she was energetic and resourceful, so that her name runs like a bright thread through all his writing: always "Emma assisting" whether planting potatoes, or building a stone wall, or digging dock root, or riding six miles to get a needed tool, or baking half the night to be ready with food for the visits of the authorities.

Emma was content in Harmony; she kept her quarters clean and attractive, and looked forward to a home of her own later. Up to this time, John D. Lee had carried on his activities with no fear of being called to account for the massacre at the Mountain Meadows. But in May 1859, he had word that a group of officers and soldiers were on the track of all those who had been in any way connected with that tragedy. Together with Philip Klingonsmith, who was already in hiding in the same general area, Lee went across the valley to the bluffs east of the farm where with his field glass he could see the family about their duties.

Each evening two or three of his wives would meet him with food at an appointed place, visit with him, and tell him the news, then one would remain overnight while the others returned to the home.

Emma was far advanced in her first pregnancy, so it was impossible for her to come out. She told herself that perhaps a letter would be better than a visit because John could read it over and over and keep it for years. She was right. He copied the letter into his journal, where the first part was preserved. The end was lost with a missing section. The entry read:

> Emma, my English girl, sent me a letter the better to express her feelings, as she was unable to come, expecting to be confined soon. The few words are as follows: My Dear Companion—It affords me joy that I cannot express to know that you are alive and have been safely delivered from the hands of your enemies thus far, who have been hunting you like a rowe on the mountain for the Kingdom of Heaven's sake. Yet I cannot but feel melancholy at times when I think of the sufferings and hardships that you must necessarily undergo in the mountains; saying nothing about the society of your family whom you love as dear as life. My prayers for your deliverance and safe return to the bosom of your family who loves you dear, has been unceasing. And although I cannot be with you in person to share your sorrows, yet the Lord knows that I am in spirit, and I also bear testimony that your spirit visits us. May God speedily permit you to return home, for I feel as though I could not stay from you much longer. I am sometimes tempted to try to climb the mountains in search of you. God bless you, my dear, to live long on the earth to bless and enjoy the society. . . . [remainder missing]

By May 23 Lee was home. He reported: "Today planted potatoes. Shell Stoddard took dinner with me, it being the first meal that I have eat in my house in 4 weeks."

We must look also in Lee's journal for the account of Emma's delivery:

> On Thursday morning [June 30, 1859] at 1 o'clock, Emma, my seventeenth wife, was delivered of a still born son. The child was large and proper but the mother was hurt in a fall some days before its birth, which was supposed to be the cause of its death. By its mother's request I gave it the name of John Henry, after her father and myself. At 10 a.m. its remains was neatly interred in the Harmony grave yard.

All through the summer, Lee had not only his family but also many hired hands busy at harvesting, plowing, ditching, building, repairing. In early August he decided to take a four-horse team and visit his friends in Pocketville. Along for company were Emma, and the newlyweds, John Alma and Mary Ann. On the way they were to gather dock root for the tannery.

The melons were ripe and plentiful; there were patches of wild dock root for the digging. Lee's record summarizes it. "Frid., Augt. 12th [1859], diging D[o]ck Root. Supped at Riggs' & Pollock's. Reac[h]ed home about Sunset, brought with us 12 bushels Doc. Root & 25 Mellons. I agreed to give My Son Alma the best Mare & colt that I owned out of Some 20 head & let Him visit 8 days, provide[d] he would leve of[f] the use of Tobacco."

Perhaps because of the loss of her baby, Emma was taken along on many of his trips. She was so industrious, so eager to improve the living standard. For example, she took the wool to the upper stream to wash it and spread it out to dry, picking and cleaning it of burrs and sticks and dirt, getting it ready for carding, a three-day task.

In September of 1859, she proved her value on the road. Lee recorded:

> I started to Washington with 500 feet Flooring, Provisions, Boilers &c. for Manufacturing Molasses. Emma, one of my wives, [with me] . . . At the dis.[tance] of 8 ms. Encamped for the Night.

Thurs., 22nd. Resumed our travel. The roads being Rough & load
heavy, I broke 4 spokes in one of [the] wheels, which forced me to leve
my lumber, & at the distance of 6 ms. further My hind Ex. broke down.
Emma took one of the Horses & Rode to Toquerville dis. 4 ms. &
brought Some augurs. Spliced the Ex & Roled on. . . .

The year 1859 closed with another wedding in the Lee family; Lee's
daughter Mary Adoline was married to Marcus Darrow. This meant
Emma would be in charge of the food department. What to serve was
decided by a general discussion, but preparation, organization, and
general direction seemed to fall naturally to Emma. She accepted it
willingly, because it was her responsibility; and she knew that her husband really appreciated it. Lee had made a special trip to Cedar City
to secure necessary items for the party, and while there he gave oral
invitations to more than twenty-five people. They would be guests in
his home on Christmas Eve and on Sunday, which was Christmas Day.
Of the affair, Lee wrote in his diary:

Sat., Dec. 24th. At 12 noon Bishop Lunt & suite arrived in good
Spirits. Their Horses & themselves were all Entertained at my Mansion at my expense. At 1 p.m. the Party Dined. I also furnished 18$
worth of Spirits. After dinner the dancing commenced & at 8 o'clock
Eve, my Daughter Mary Adoline, by Aggathean was Married to
Marcus Henry Darrow, a young Man about 22 years of age. The Right
of Matrimony was Solmnised by Bishop H. Lunt. Super at 9. The
Dancing broke up at 2 morn. The Guest & all Enjoyed themselves to
the hilt. Not the lest Particle of feelings or disorder was seen, heard,
or felt by any presant.

Most of the visitors remained over Sunday and attended meeting
before returning. As they left, they invited Lee to bring his family to
Cedar City to return the visit. This he did within the week, taking
Caroline and Emma, both of whom had special friends there. Emma
and Elizabeth Haight needed little entertaining. The chance to be
together by themselves was enough, for they could discuss their private
affairs: their husbands, their relationship with the other wives, the fact
that Emma had lost a child, and that neither was pregnant now. They
were agreed that to have a baby or two or three would be life's greatest
blessing, a blessing that Elizabeth would never enjoy.

The Lee family looked forward to the year 1860 with expectation. The work in Washington had been most rewarding; the rock mansion was occupied and comfortable, though there was some finishing work to be done. In order to take advantage of the climate there, Lee went down on New Year's Day and the next night entertained the Mormon Seventies in his social hall at a party which was a mixture of meeting and celebrating.

During the week he purchased all of Brother Theodore Turley's property, which included his blacksmith shop and equipment, also a fine set of carpenter tools. How important good tools were! They made the difference between beautiful work and makeshift jobs.

After two weeks in Washington, he returned to Harmony for a few days to look after things in general. When he again traveled back to Washington, he took along Rachel and Emma—Rachel to stay in the mild climate until her confinement and Emma for general help, inside the home and out.

Lee set out trees, he paved his front water ditch, he worked on a stone wall the full width of his property, and he put up a picket gate at the entrance, which Emma painted a peach color.

Most important, Brother Walter Dodge introduced him to the "living fence," which became a pattern for all southern Utah. This was made by setting out cottonwood or willow saplings or just cuttings three to six inches in diameter and three to four feet tall. Set into the ground a foot or so and kept damp, they would take root and grow into a solid, living fence. They should be placed far enough apart for the trunks to reach maturity. Topped after a few years of growth, they would produce firewood annually.

Rachel's baby was born March 9, and she felt that she would not have survived the ordeal without the help of her husband.

The census taker did not reach Harmony until midsummer. Emma was evidently cooking for all the farm help, at least ten men, since they were listed under her "domicile." Some of the men were still at work for Lee two years later.

As for Emma, her event of the year was the birth of a second son on December 16, 1860, "a proper child, 9½ pounds." Her joy was full. She called him William James, which soon became Bill or Billy for short.

On February 7, as Lee was at work on his mill in Washington, word came that Brothers George A. Smith and Joseph A. Young had arrived at his home there and wished to see him. They greeted him heartily, informed him that on their way down they had also put up at his home in Harmony, where Emma had prepared the meals. So as they could see, all was well there. In the evening, a meeting was held in Lee's Social Hall, it being the largest room in Washington.

The next morning Lee rode with them to show his small flour mill, his molasses-making setup, his tannery pond. They seemed much impressed and "promised me that all the opposition that is now against me will turn to my good & will ultimately give me the More influence &c."

Lee did not go with the visitors to Santa Clara, but they returned Sunday evening. Bishop Covington, Dudley Leavitt, and Andrew Gibbons all joined them at the Lee home for breakfast, and Lee himself went on with the group up the river to the settlements there. They visited Toquerville, Grafton, and Pocketville, preaching as they went about the state of the Union and the Civil War as heralding the Last Days and the triumph of Israel.

Lee went as far north with the company as Cedar City, then returned to take a load of provisions to Washington. For all the praise that he had received from the brethren here, he later learned that at a meeting of Brother George A. Smith with the authorities at Parowan, he alone had been named as having been in the vicinity at the time of the Mountain Meadows Massacre. Isaac C. Haight and Philip Klingonsmith, both of whom had left the area, were dropped from their public offices. William H. Dame was cleared at his insistence that all the High Council sign a written statement to that effect. He declared loudly that if they dared to implicate him in the massacre, he would quickly put the saddle onto the right horse—George A. Smith, himself, who sat among them. It had been he who had stirred up the war spirit.

Back in Washington through the mild spring weather, Lee was finishing his mill, transplanting the fruit trees of last year's pits, and putting up a neat backhouse with a shingle roof. For Emma, this was the best mark of civilization. Across the plains, it had been "gents to the right and ladies to the left" and seek your own cover. After the first

home shelters were built, the outhouse was often a rickety affair, sometimes only four posts set into the ground and an old canvas nailed
around three sides, with a loose front of canvas to fasten on a nail. Now
here was one with a board floor, good seats, two larger ones and one
little child-size, and an overhanging shingle roof. This was quality,
indeed, good enough for the use of Brother Brigham himself; though,
of course, he would have the commode in his bedroom for night use.

All this spring, Lee had a large crew at work, on the mill, at the
blacksmith shop, and clearing new land near Toquerville, where he had
staked out 250 to 300 acres of the best quality.

Lee had parted with George A. Smith and his party in mid–March.
Now, scarcely two months later, Brother Brigham followed, eager to see
for himself the conditions of the south. On May 28 his company of
twenty-three carriages and seventy persons stopped at Lee's home in
Washington. Lee names them all in his diary. Learning that they were
on their way, Lee sent to Harmony for his Queensware china to furnish
the table. He had some necessary items of food brought also, that he
might do justice to his visitors.

Lee provided forty of the seventy people with sleeping accommodations, and all ate supper and breakfast at his table.

As always, Emma was chief manager in the kitchen, for her little
Bill, now past five months old, was healthy and good-natured. She was
proud to show him to President Young, who remembered her very well
indeed and congratulated her on the whole setup, so different from the
one of which she had complained.

During his visit to the experimental cotton farms and his survey of
the area as a whole, Brigham Young was so impressed that he returned,
and at the October conference following, he called 300 families to go
south and settle St. George.

He directed the Swiss emigrants to settle the Santa Clara area to
plant orchards and vineyards, to produce wine, since a few of them were
experienced vintners.

The people responded immediately, many of them arriving in early
November, and all of them there before Christmas. None had moved
onto their grounds as yet; they were waiting for a survey to be made.
On Christmas Eve a storm set in. It was general, all over the area, but

Harmony, being higher in the mountains and on a northeast location, got more than its share. The detailed account of the Ward Record is eloquent:

> Sunday, Dec. 29, 1861. Meeting in Prest. J. D. Lee's family hall at 10 a.m. Through the week the storms still raging; prospects dark and gloomy; the Earth a sea of water and thus closes 1861.
>
> Jany. 1st, 1862. Begins with a storm. The face of the country is deluged with water.
>
> Sat., Jan. 4, 1862. Snow about 8 inches deep. Fort Harmony [built, as were the houses, chiefly of adobe brick] is almost decomposed and returned back to its native element.
>
> Elder Lee and a portion of his family have suffered severely during the storm as they were trying to make shelters at their new location: the water in their underground rooms raised to a depth of 3 feet, Bailing night and day, but unable to keep it out and were at last compelled to abandon them and take the storm in shantys made of planks; (wind shifted North). During the entire storm the wind was south but when it changed the weather became severe, yet they thought better to suffer than to risk being buried up alive in Fort Harmony.
>
> Harmony.Teus. 7, 1863[2]. Snowy through the day.
>
> Thurs., Jany. 9, 1862. Snow 10 inches deep.
>
> Sunday, Jany. 13, 1862. The storm still raging, spreading a mantle of gloom over Harmony, the walls of which are constantly crumbling down, rendering the houses actually dangerous altho a short time previous Prest. B. Young said it was the best Fort ever built in the Territory; instead of meeting, Prest. Lee sumoned another portion of his family to the upper place. About 9 at night a dreadful snow storm on them.
>
> Monday, Jany. 14, 1862. The storm most vehemently raging. About 1 p.m. Prest. Lee's barn fell, the side had been washed out several days before and the timbers alone supported it; Several Horses, Calves, and hogs were in it when it fell but nothing was hurt.
>
> The S. side is expected to fall before morning. The Pres. removed the remainder of his family on the west line and spent another night of gloom and darkness; parts of walls constantly falling. This was a time of watching as well as praying, for there was a prospect of being buried

in masses of ruins; about midnight a part of the South wall fell with an awful crash. Killed 2 chickens only. At length daylight came. Storm still raging.

Sat., Jan. 18 [19], 1862. Pres. Lee through the kindness of Wm. and Harvey A. Pace, also Geo. M. Sevy, manned 3 wagons with 8 yoke of catle to each wagon (as the axle tree would in places drag the ground) and removed all the families from the Fort except Sarah C. Lee and family. Her house was considered safe and the only place of refuge where all the families staid the night previous; the storm unabating, Pres. Lee was 8 days without undressing or putting on dry clothes. The families were removed through the storm, women and children soaking wet.

Reports say that the Rio Virgin and Santa Clara rivers were overflowing the country and doing much damage. The mill of Jacob Hamblin's and City were washed away, orchards and vineyards desolated. The towns of Adventure, Rockville, Grafton, and Pocketville were all destroyed. Bishop P. K. Smith of Adventure had his house, Cane mill, Blacksmith shop, 150 Gals. molasses and much of his household and kitchen furniture was down the flood. Bishop N. C. Tenney lost his houses and furniture and loosing a part of his family.

Monday, Jany. 27, 1862. Cloudy. W. N. Evening, commenced snowing. Through the night, fell 6 inches deep.

Wen., Jany. 29, 1862, snow 8 inches.

Thurs., Jan. 30, 1862. Rather mild. Rain through the night reduced the snow to 4 inches.

Friday, Jany. 31, 1862. This morning the sun was seen for the first time in 28½ days. At 1 commenced snowing again.

Thurs., Feb. 6th, 1862. Snowing about 10 a.m. Stacked up. Snow about 10 inches. About 1 W. shifted S.E. to N. Cold and cutting. The President had all his family removed except Caroline. Wagons and Teams were all got ready to remove them on the 7th. They would have been removed before had not Sarah Caroline insisted to remain a few days longer to finish up her spinning. Felt there could be no danger as the roof was removed and the rain ceased. Yet the President said that it was not agreeable with his feelings for them to remain there. About dark the mother felt impressed to leave the room. While in the act of making up her bed, leaving the clothes in a chair,

took Terressa with her and the two older children, leaving the youngest in. When a few places from the door, a sudden gust of wind dashed
from the N., through [threw] down a single partition wall into the
floor and broke through to the lower floor, killing of the little children,
little Geo. A. and Margarett Ann. The other two each was at the feet
of the two that was killed. A shocking and sad occurrence—the father
and mother had both been warned of it previous.

Through it all, Emma was calm. Yes, it was cold and uncomfort-
able, but really not bitter cold; and they were not hungry. The body
can survive cold if it has food to keep its inner fires burning. At the
"Misery Camp" with the handcart company she had promised the Dear
Lord that if she could survive this ordeal, she would never complain of
the weather again as long as she lived. Now was a good time to keep
that promise, and she did it by being cheerful and uncomplaining, seeing that everyone had food and such wraps and shelter as were available.

The deaths of little George A. and Margarett Ann were indeed a
tragedy; it should be a lesson to every person to heed the promptings of
the spirit and act quickly. As for the children themselves, the sweet little
things went instantly without fear or pain—transported into another
life in the twinkling of an eye. They would be happy in their new home.

Though Emma said nothing about her past experience with the
handcart company, she lived it through in her mind constantly: a tiny
starved-to-death baby was wrapped tightly in its shawl and placed
carefully on top of the growing pile of bodies; yet it was easy to understand when some desperate person unwrapped it and took the shawl
away. It might help to save someone's life. She herself had removed
the shoes, coat, and pants from the body of a man with the thought
that they might help a living person to survive through the long time of
waiting for relief. Yes, through this present period of suffering, Emma
endeared herself to every member of the Lee family.

The storm finally did end, and spring came. Though Lee had lost
heavily here, it was nothing compared to what had happened to his
holdings in Washington. His flour mill was gone entirely as was his
molasses mill, for both were in the valley. He was using the fall in the
stream for power to run the flour mill; and the low, grassy area just
below it a few rods was an ideal place for stacking the cane, for

running it through the rollers, and for cooking it in the long tin boiler. Everything was gone, washed out slick and clean; buried in the debris miles below.

Lee could be thankful that his mansion stood proud and beautiful behind the rock fence with the painted gate; the yard, the corrals, the fishpond, and the young trees all survived, as did the outhouse. He should be thankful for these things, he knew, yet he did have a severe cutback in business. The value of the blacksmith tools purchased from Brother Turley could hardly be measured in money, and they, too, were gone.

Worse than that was the attitude of Erastus Snow toward him— a coldness that meant no communication whatever on any matter. Brother Brigham had brought visiting crowds to Lee's homes both at Harmony and Washington until Erastus had his Big House in St. George finished, where Brigham Young made his headquarters until his own Winter Home could be completed.

By 1861 every man who had been at Mountain Meadows on that bloody, terrible day in 1857 had left the area. Some were in Arizona, others out in Nevada at Panaca or Pioche, still others on lonely ranches beyond Kanab. That Lee should remain and carry on business as before, going to church and participating in civic affairs, seemed to irritate Brother Snow. Lee, pretending not to notice, went ahead and finished Emma's small home on the upper site where she had wanted it, gave her her own garden, pigs, chickens, cow, arranged for her to board the hired men, and in general carried on his regular pattern of life.

Just before Billy's third birthday, a new brother was born on November 29, 1863. He, too, was a husky, healthy lad, who was named Isaac Lee and called Ike. How wonderful to have two little boys to grow up together!

For almost three years Emma continued to live in her small two-room home high above all the other houses, to board the hired men, to come down to the mansion when important company arrived to help with the cooking, and to always be depended upon for making the pastry.

When, early in the spring of 1866, Lee arrived home with another wife, Emma, then pregnant, understood how Aggatha must have felt whenever he added another to the household. Ann Gordge was very young, just going on seventeen; she was tall and lithe and beautiful.

Emma lost her temper with the new wife one day, reproving her sharply. Ann paid back in kind until five-year-old Billy ran for his father to come and settle the dispute before the women hurt each other. Lee separated them and reproved them both sharply, as well as the elder wife Terressa Chamberlain, who should have used her influence earlier toward a quiet settlement of the differences between the two girls.

The result was the addition of another large room for Ann to have her own private place, though the women shared the kitchen and cellar.

Emma kept thinking about the birth of her new baby, and one day she and Rachel were visiting about their families. The fact came up that Rachel had borne three girls and no sons, while Emma had given birth to three boys. "Well, Rachel, if this next one is a boy, I'll give it to you," Emma said in a spirit of bravado. Her husband rebuked her for such a wicked statement.

"You are carrying not only a baby girl, but twin girls, and the name of the first shall be Rachel Emma, for you two sitting here, and the second born shall be Ann Eliza, for your companion wife and your friend Elizabeth Summers with whom you traveled the first part of your trip to Zion. I cannot promise that you will be able to keep both these little girls because of your rebellious spirit and caustic tongue. You yourself will be most responsible for the outcome."

There seemed to be many changes and tensions in the Lee family that year. In May 1866 Aggatha, who had been ill, became worse. The family gathered; they used all their known remedies together with faith and prayers and administration, but on June 4, 1866, she died, and of necessity was buried the next day. Lee wrote a detailed account of all the activities—the persons who built the coffin and decorated it, those who prepared the grave, and those who in song or speech contributed to the service. He added, that Emma and those of her household prepared dinner for all those who assisted in any way.

Emma had been keenly touched when she came to bid Aggatha good-bye, and the dying woman said to her, "God bless you to keep both your little daughters," for she too knew of Lee's prediction.

On Sunday, July 22, 1866, John D. Lee wrote in his diary:

Emma B., my 16th in the covenant, who was confined & according to previous promises that I made to her, brought fourth a pair of twin Girls, one of which was Named before its birth, that is, the first Born was called Rachel Emma & the other was called Ana Eliza. They were born about 4 p.m. & about 30 minets between the Births (4 to 4:30 m.). The children were proper & lively, though one of them was badly wraped & was near smothering. One of them weighed 8½ lls., the 2nd, A.E. 8¾, making 17¼ lls. Witnesses were presant who bore testimony of the promised children. . . .

Lee's record during the year 1866 is quite full and complete, but concerned mostly with business transactions, trading, buying and selling, improving and enlarging his holdings not only in the Harmony area but in Kanarraville and Washington as well. He made repeated trips to Cedar City and Parowan, preaching in Sunday services wherever he happened to be, and carried on as though nothing had happened. He did take time out, however, to record the birth of Ann's first child. "Harmony. Thurs., March 14th, 1867. At 5 o'c. morning Ann Gordge was delivered of a son, weighed 10 lls. Named it Sam[u]el James for her father & uncle. Ann E. Imlay, Midwife. To day I made a Pair of shoes, repared a spring wheel, Made a Pair of swifts, put leads [lids?] to two Boxes &c."

By this time there were cordial relations between Emma and Ann; Emma's twin girls, now eight months old, were healthy and good-natured, while six-year-old Billy was a good errand boy and helper with the chores, with Ike following along eager to help, too.

Lee's diary through these years is very detailed, recording his busy, active business life. Upon returning home from a fruitful trip, April 11, 1867, he found among his mail a mission call for Aggatha's two oldest sons, Joseph Hyrum and John Willard—shortened to Joseph and Willard. This was news, indeed, for to send one missionary out was a family drain. But two! The boys were young, Joseph was twenty-three and Willard was nearly nineteen; they had been raised on the frontier with only a little formal education. A mission would, in a way, be the best education they could get, for they would put their whole time to study of the Scriptures and presenting their own special version.

They would drive a herd of cattle to Salt Lake City to sell, enough for all their expenses. On April 25 the herd started, driven by the two boys, while their father followed in a wagon, accompanied by Emma and the twin girls. Emma was elated! She could hardly believe that she could have her husband all to herself for so long a time. And she could visit her sister, Fanny, and shop in the city.

Soon after they were on their way, they had met President Young and Lee had indicated that he thought the boys would do better in England than in the Southern States Mission. He was pleased when President Young agreed.

Best of all, Lee secured from Bishop H. Lunt the following: "To Pres. B. Young & Council & to all Saints; I hereby certify that Bro. J. D. Lee is a staunch, firm Latter day Saint, seeks to build up the Kingdom of God & live by its Principles & is in full faith and Fellowship. Signed, Bishop H. Lunt."

This was most important, for it gave him a warm welcome wherever he went to trade. He carried it with him always, showing it to each person with whom he had dealings.

On Monday, May 13, they arrived at the city. They sold their beef cattle to Brother "Ferramore Litle" who treated them to beer, and then served them a sumptuous dinner, for he had the name of having the best table of any in the city. Later, they located Emma's sister Fanny Gilbert. The two had not seen each other for twelve years. Lee made no remarks about Fanny's husband, but she herself was at the washtub, making her living by doing people's laundry. No other details except that "the children all fondled on their uncle as though they had been raised with me, or I their Father."

The next day, Brigham Young and party arrived back in Salt Lake City from their trip south, and Lee was much impressed at the welcome Young received.

An Escort of about 25,000 Persons, making about 5 miles long, consisting of the Military in uniform with the various Brass & Martial Bands, drawn by Matched Horses, from 4 to 8 to each veacle, to geather with the Juveniles, about 24 companies headed by their respective Teachers each bearing Banners with mottoes emblematic of their grades & positions in the church. Also the military on foot, next the citizens in mass, comprising an Escort of about 25 thousand. Each passed in review before their President's Mansion, who had assended to the Balastrade of the same, where he stood for near 1¾ of an hour bowing or with a wave of the hand or hat acknowledged their respect, & not until the last company had passed, did he stop to embrace his Family. . . .

The next day Joseph and Willard received their anointings and were set apart for their missions. Their father made arrangements for them to travel with a wagon train east and earn their way by helping on the road. Each carried $100.00 in cash in addition to new outfits of clothing. They parted in tears, especially Willard, who asked his father's forgiveness for his past rebellious spirit.

Emma wished to help by taking three of her sister's children— Henry, Joseph, and Elizabeth, back south where they could remain until fall. The idea was that they might be help enough to earn their keep.

The trip home was uneventful and the fact that Emma's two little boys had learned that the travelers were near and had walked more than three miles out to meet them thrilled their mother to tears. John was pleased to find conditions on his farm much better than he had expected for which he praised the Lord.

Emma did not dream of the complications which would develop when she brought her sister's three children down to stay the summer of 1867. Henry was old enough to do a man's work, but he was a constant worry; he was seized by fits of insanity or "possessed of an evil spirit" some thought. At any rate, he was unpredictable, running away for days at a time. Joseph and Elizabeth, on the other hand, were willing and cheerful helpers in such chores and housework as they could do. But Emma was relieved when they were safely home with their mother again.

Lee at once set about to check on his wide holdings. He found Mary Leah at Toquerville cold and rebellious. She had made a complaint to Erastus Snow charging Lee with neglect. This was the beginning of the end of their marital relations. On the other hand, his family at Washington was in the midst of a party, to which he was most cordially welcomed. "The Behavior & Training of my children here reflects credit on their Mothers," he wrote.

However, it was evident that sentiment was building up against Lee in many quarters. He was just too prosperous, and he had too many thrifty holdings in too many places. The first difficulty occurred when Emma brought a letter from the post office: "The author styeling himself MaJ. Burt . . . giving me 10 days to make my escape in or I should be hung up in that old Fort Harmony for being in the Mountain Meadow Massacre. . . ." Lee was absent when it came but recorded the details on April 11, 1868.

> Emma accused Georgee Hicks & Jno. Lawson of Fabricating the Letter, thinking to freighting us; & that he was a poor sneaking pusylanimous Pup & always Medling with other men's Matter & that he had better sing low & keep out of her Path or she would put a load of salt in his Backside. . . . This Hicks was a Traitor & Pointed out all the Brethrn who he thought had been at Mountain Meadow when Indians killed them to the Gentiles. He prefered a charge against Emma for UnChristianlike conduct before Bishop W. D. Pace. It was proven before the court that Hicks had provoked Emma by a Train of abuse to say what she did. The decission was that Ema & [Hicks?] Should be rebaptised . . . & that Hicks & I should make Friends & I agred to meet him 2½ of the way but he refused. . . . I said it was rather hard to require a woman to be rebaptised for . . . defending her Husband against the insults & abuse of Traitor. . . . Emma asked the prevelege of choice in the man to Baptise her. The Bishop granted it. She says, I am much obliged. I demand Baptism at your hands, seeing that you are so inconsiderate as to require a woman to be immersed when the water is full of snow & Ice & that too for defending the rights of her husband. You should pay a litle of [the] penalty for making such a descision & perhaps if your back side gets wet in Ice water you will be more careful how you decide again. The majority of the People said, Stick him to it, Emma, it is but Just. But the Bishop made an Excuse to go to Kannara & got out of it.

The year 1868 was one of prosperity for the Lee family: building, improving, setting up a new bee culture, and planting mulberry trees with a thought of silk-raising. There had been no fear of officers and no serious impediments to his business; John D. moved among his families freely.

Since the death of Aggatha, Emma and Ann had lived together and had grown very fond of one another. The fact that Terressa lived in the same house helped to draw them nearer, for their interests were different from hers. Ann named her little daughter Merabe Emma, for her mother and sister wife, but somehow the nickname "Belle" was adopted; folklore says that it was because she was such a pretty child that her father once called her "the belle of the ball." Nicknames were often adopted without reason, so Belle's older brother became Jimmie or "Jim Gribble."

In early 1869 Brother Brigham started to visit the settlements to the south, but at Fillmore his group was overtaken by a snowstorm. By now the new telegraph line was in operation to Cedar City, so word went out that President Young could not tell exactly when he would arrive.

On Monday evening, April 26, 1869, Young's caravan pulled in at the home of John D. Lee at Harmony, eight carriages in all. In his characteristic way, John D. Lee recorded those he considered important in the order of their positions: Brother Brigham had his twenty-fifth wife, Mary Van Cott, as well as Brigham Young, Jr., and an unnamed son; also Dunsford and wife, Susa Young; plus two additional daughters. More important to Lee were Daniel H. Wells and Louisa Free, who had previously been Lee's favorite wife, John Taylor, George Q. Cannon, W. "Woodrough" and lady, and Horace S. Eldridge and wife.

At leaving the next morning the President made a special request that John D. tuck a fox-skin around him and at this time told him when the group would arrive in Washington. Lee understood his message and acted. With some awe, Lee concluded his account of the encounter. "The two Briggs [i.e., Brigham Young, Sr., and Brigham Young, Jr.] were side by side in the Same Carriage, the Father & son weighing near 500 lbs."

Early on Thursday morning, Lee was in Washington to make preparations for meeting the President. In the late afternoon an escort of horsemen under Captain W. Freeman rode out a mile or so and waited until sunset, then returned home with the excuse that the President would not be out traveling that late. In less than half an hour the company arrived, and Brother Brigham asked Lee sharply, "Where was your escort?" Lee apologized, saying that if he had been in charge, this would not have happened.

Then the President asked especially if Lee could provide sleeping quarters for him and his wife and two younger daughters; for he was weary after driving thirty miles over that rough road. Brother Wells and the others were sent to the home of Bishop Covington to be assigned out from there. Lee was proud to hear the President say, "Bishop, I will come back and take a bowl of mush and milk with you tonight & will breakfast with Brother Lee."

The next morning the President was welcomed by the townspeople of Washington: groups of children carried mottoes, the first being WELCOME BRIGHAM, THE FRIEND OF MANKIND. The cotton mill was run a few minutes in his honor. The Santa Clara Brass Band and the St. George Military Band met him.

At this point, the President suggested that Lee go back to Washington, which John D. understood was Brother Brigham's way to appease Erastus Snow. So he immediately returned to Washington and gathered up his family to come to the conference, which was held in the basement of the new Tabernacle under construction in St. George. Lee sat near the back of the hall, and took careful minutes of the meetings, filling his handbook.

Lee had misgivings about the visit for though Brother Brigham in private had been warm and friendly, in public he had avoided Lee entirely. The President returned north by way of Pine Valley and Pinto.

In early September of 1869, John D. Lee decided to build a nice large house for his wives Emma and Ann, but there was much to be done in preparation for it. He needed a lime kiln with an abundant amount of lime properly burned; this was a necessity. His record says: "Nov. 2nd. We started up the Kanyon; Emma went with me to cook for us. On the 8th inst. we finish the Kiln & returned Home with a load of Lime drawn by 4 Mules & Horses. In the Mean time my teams & Boys hauled 10 loads of wood home besides 15 cords for the kiln."

On October 20 the Navajoes made a raid on the settlements and drove off about 1,000 head of horses and mules. Some were recovered, but by November 9, Lee had recovered only a few. "I have lost 25 to 40 head," he wrote. Among them, "some valuable horses of fine Blood, worth from 2 to $300 a Peace."

> Teus., Nov. 9th, 1869. Today I commenced laying the Brick in My large dwelling for Emma & Ann. . . .
>
> Thurs., Nov. 11th. I am getting on finely with my Mason work, also with the hauling of My Brick & sand. To day Emma B. had a quilting & a sumptuous Dinner. John Sevy pushing the Door and window fraims. I also sent Jos. H. to Mill with a load of grain. . . .
>
> 25th. Quite cool. To day we run up 2 chimys to the square.
>
> 26th. Jos. Worthen came & worked ½ day on an other chimny. . . . John David, My son by Lovina V. Y., arrived from washington for a load of Potatoes.

On November 29, 1869, John Lawson and his son-in-law George Dodds came onto Lee's property and proceeded to chop out the growth of young trees along the ditch bank. Lee stopped them and ordered them off his property. They threatened each other with guns, but Lawson went right on chopping. Then Lee took Lawson's ax away from him and held it, expecting to go the next morning for a writ from a justice of the peace. But Lawson came again early the next morning when Emma and Ann were alone on the place. Hearing the cutting going on, the women went out to stop it, Emma with a pan of hot water. At the first dash, Lawson said, "Pour it on!" Ann came out of her door with another dose, and while he was paying attention to her, Emma came in from the other side, threw her pan, and jumped to catch his arm that held the ax, tripping him onto his back.

"He is trying to kill me with his ax," Emma shouted, wherewith Ann threw her second load of water and leaped upon him also. Lee wrote:

> When I with several others reached the scene of action, found them both on the ground & Ann with one hand in his hair & with the other pounding him in the face. In the mean time Emma returnd with a New Supply of hot watter & then pitched into him with Ann & they bothe handled him rather Ruff. His face was a gore of Blood. My Son Willard finally took them off of him. He then presistd until I took his ax away & sent it to the House. . . . But in stead of waiting for Me to take out a writt for him for Tresspass & damage, he went to

Kannarrah, in his Blood without washing & complained upon Oath & took out a writ for Me & my wives Emma & Ann for assault & Battering & with attempt to Kill. . . .

Lee's son-in-law M. H. Darrow, Sheriff, served the writ, notifying John D., Emma, and Ann to appear before Justices Pollock and Martingale, on Saturday, December 4, 1869, at Kanarraville. The witnesses were examined. Bishop L. W. Roundy sat on the case and fined John Lawson and said that Lee was justified in defending his rights.

During the winter, Lee worked some on his "new brick mansion," and before spring Emma and Ann moved in, though all the last finishing was not done. All the fireplaces working, the shingle roof waterproofed, and a solid new floor with handmade rugs and carpet strips combined to make the women content. Terressa could have the little house they had vacated, and her son Charles could sleep in the other bedroom.

The Big Move

Emma and Ann were both pleased with their setup in the new brick house. They cooperated to make it as pleasant and comfortable as they could and also managed to have a good vegetable garden, producing more than they needed. So Emma asked Aunt Kisiah Redd if she would be willing to do some sewing in exchange for fresh vegetables, fresh hot cross buns or bread or fancy decorated cakes. In this way Emma and Ann were able to get items that they could never have paid cash for, among them brightly colored bonnets for themselves and all three little girls.

On August 15, 1870, John D. Lee entered in the record: "My crop was Excellent both of vegatables, Fruit & grain. I had My Wheat thrashed & Binned in the Mo. of August. I had 400 Bushels of Wheat. The Production of my Farm this season amounted to over $4000."

The next day Lee received a message from President Brigham Young, asking Lee to join his party on an exploring expedition up through the mountains to the headwaters of the Sevier River and over onto the plateau. For twelve days John D. was gone, during which time he kept a careful record of the trip. Upon his arrival home he called the family together and told them: "I shall not go into any detail about our trip, except to tell you that we must sell all our holdings here, in Kanarraville, and Washington, and move out to the headwaters on the Paria. There we will set up on a large tract of grazing land. We must lose no time if we get set up for the winter." He acted promptly, as his diary shows:

> Tokerville. Wed., Sept. 12th [14th], 1870. Reached home about 3 p.m. Offered my Farm at N. Harmony for sale. In the meantime Got in my corn, Potatoes, &cc., & worked up cane. Had about 400 Gallons Molasses. Dried, & let out on shares to dry, as Much of My Fruit as I could. Sold 8 acres of land to Bishop W. D. Pace for $400, 4 acres to W. Brinner for $200 cash & the remander of My Farm to L. H. Redd for four thousand five hundred dollars, $3000 payable in horn stock, the remaining $1500 payable in wheat at Tithing Price in yearly instalments of $500 each.

The Lee family all took comfort in the knowledge that they would be working with Levi Stewart, for they had all heard often of how Brother Stewart had brought John D. Lee the *Book of Mormon* by which he was converted; how together they had traveled with their families to the Far West to meet the Prophet, how they stood side by side during the terrible hardships that followed. It was no surprise to them that when Brother Brigham asked Levi to set up a sawmill on the mountain where there were forests unlimited, he should answer: "I will take it over if you will ask John D. Lee to work with me. We have worked together before, and Brother Lee is a good hand with machinery."

With such prospects, the Lee family were all comforted about the move. What they did not know was their husband and father had been officially excommunicated from the Church on October 8, 1870. He did not receive the notice himself until November 18.

In the meantime, they had their sawmill set up and running, but it ran only a short time before a part was broken; with the distances as they were, they would be delayed some weeks.

Then a terrible calamity hit Levi Stewart's home in Kanab. A fire which consumed the whole fort took six members of his family including his wife, leaving Stewart prostrated to the point that he himself died in less than six months.

Soon after that, Lee received notice of his being dropped from the Church, so he made a trip to St. George in December where he called on Brigham Young. President Young was cordial and told him that the action had been necessary; the President continued that he himself was loyal in his love for Lee and would do all he could for him.

Lee stayed with the wives in Washington and called on those at Harmony; and on January 6, 1871, he started with Sarah Caroline and her family for the new settlement.

Emma and Ann had worked together through the fall and had joined in their own Christmas activities. With all the others gone, they planned their work together, also their cooking and the making of toys for the children. But with spring coming on, Emma felt that she should make up her mind. Should she follow her husband, or should she just stay in her home and claim it as her right? Busy tongues were wagging wherever she went. She knew that Bishop W. D. Pace was using his influence to keep some of the Lee boys from following their father.

How grateful she was when Aunt Kisiah Redd came to visit her! Many years ago, John D. Lee had converted Kisiah's husband and all the family to the Church; Lemuel H. Redd had been a staunch friend ever since.

"You go out and see for yourself," Aunt Kisiah said. "Don't listen to anybody else. When you meet your husband and see the situation, your own heart will tell you what to do. I can help Ann with the children while you're gone, or I can just take them over here." Emma consented.

So it was that on March 6, 1871, Emma climbed out of the wagon and ran to embrace her husband, before he knew she was coming. Aunt Kisiah was right! She did know what to do! Of course she would come out. Here were already two solid log houses up, one with a shingle roof; here was land cleared and cattle grazed on the meadowlands.

After two weeks, Emma returned to Harmony with a horse team, taking Nancy Emily, Rachel's twenty-year-old daughter, along for company. Emma and her children pulled out of Harmony on March 20, in good spring weather, knowing that the round trip would take a full month.

On their return, John D. Lee wrote:

On Meeting Jos. & Willard, they fell on My Neck, kissed Me & we wept with Joy.... Every Sweet has its Bitter ... My litle children Samuel James & Mareb Emma by Ann George [Gordge]. But the Mother with litle Albrt Doyl at her Breast.... had Made Ship wreck of her Faith ... & had squandered away hundreds of Dollars worth of Property....

Whether or not John D. Lee ever learned the truth about Ann's refusal to come out and join the family is questionable. But in his later life, Emma's son Billy told it, and Billy's wife wrote it down.

Lee was right when he said that much of his wheat, molasses, and provender had been either stolen, given away, or wasted. These things had happened but during Emma's month of absence. Ann was alone with the children, and the general attitude was that if a man apostatized or was excommunicated, his goods were fair gain to anyone who could get them. It was for this very reason that Lee himself during this same time went back to St. George and had Mormon men appear before the High Council for stealing eight head of his cows. Lee won the case and got his cattle back, but it was frankly admitted that "they would not have durst do this if Brother Lee had not been cut off the Church at the last conference."

So with Lee away and Emma also gone for a month, it is not so surprising that the boys should find only 15 of the 125 bushels of wheat Lee had left; two barrels of molasses gone; his seed potatoes all missing; a cook stove gone; two cattle stolen and butchered; turkeys, geese, and chickens all gone. Ann with her three very small children, Little Albert not yet weaned, would have little defense against these losses, since her home was high up on the hill and not close to the granary or corrals.

Any woman with a nursing child is not prone to be seeking other men, so that implication was most unjust. The facts were that Ann was ready to go along with Emma. Her furniture with Emma's was loaded and on its way in the lead wagons. Emma, with her own younger children, rode in the lead wagon and pulled out an hour or two before the others would be ready. It was better to have a little distance between the two companies, if only to cut down the dust. Billy was left to follow, with the idea that a bright ten year old might be a help to fetch and carry, and he wanted to ride on the high spring seat with his "uncle" Joseph.

They were practically ready to start when Ann in some way fell through a hole in the top of the potato pit. As she went down, her skirts were pushed up under her arms, and she could get neither up nor down. The boys thought it so funny that they nearly killed themselves laughing. Ann was not only angry and embarrassed, but she was being hurt by a jagged stick in her side. By the time they did engineer her out, she was sick with pain and disgust and they had hardly stopped laughing. Pulling her own personal trunk of clothes from the wagon, she told them to go on. She would stay here. In vain they tried to persuade her. She would go nowhere with any such dolts, such ignorant fools.

"Go on and laugh your heads off," she said, and went into the house and shut the door.

But they had been sent to bring the family, and the two older children had to go. That was the rule. In Mormondom at that time, the children, after they were weaned, belonged to the father. "Well, take them if you must, but I will not go," Ann said. It was not hard for Billy to coax little Jimmie and Belle into the wagon with him, promising that their mama would come in the other wagon.

Lee accepted the word of his sons that they could not persuade Ann to come, but without actually saying so, they left him thinking that she had probably found a younger, more desirable mate.

The fact was that she took her baby and went to the home of her brother David, who lived in Beaver. There she remained, getting what work she could until Little Albert was weaned. Then, leaving him to be a part of David's family, she made her way to Salt Lake City, where she found employment as a cook.

At the age of nine, Albert D. rejoined his mother, and they went on to Tintic, where Ann again got employment as a cook. When Ann was forty-six, she was married to Frank Kennedy, a mining engineer.

Perhaps we should round off this tragic little story by adding that after Jimmie and Belle were grown, they found their mother, went together to visit her and Albert, their brother. They corresponded with her as long as she lived.

Meanwhile, back at camp, John D. Lee took time to sit with both the children on his knee; he loved them and talked to them and told them what pretty children they were and how proud he was to be their father.

"Your mama couldn't come, and we are sorry about that, but we'll all love you here and take care of you."

Later, talking to Emma and Rachel separately, he told them essentially the same thing: "I grew up an unwanted child in a home, and I know what it is like. It really does something to you, to your basic character. I have only the vaguest memory of my mother, lying pale and sick on a couch. I loved the colored nurse who took care of me, though she spoke French. She really loved me too—had an interest in me. Then when Grandpa Doyle died, I was sent to my mother's sister, Aunt Charlotte, who already had more children than she wanted. I always felt in the way—or out of place. I just didn't belong. Never a good word. Never a word of praise, no matter what I did. Never a bit of affection. I tell you, I don't want these children to have it that way. If I pay some especial attention to them, you will know the reason why. I'm trying to make up for their mother. And I'll appreciate it if you will both remember this. Be kind to them."

During the summer, Lee made another trip to Dixie on business with the Stake High Council, all of whom supported him in getting back the eight head of cattle that had been stolen. His families at Washington were just getting ready to move, so Lee, traveling ahead, invited Lavina and her son David to stop with him at Skutumpah when they arrived.

By November Lee decided to make deeds of his property to his five remaining wives, Rachel Woolsey, Polly and Lavina Young, Sarah C. Williams, and Emma Batchelor. As affairs changed and new possibilities developed, there might need to be some adjustments, but each of these five was secure in receiving one-fifth of what he had.

Soon Sarah Caroline took her share and moved to Panguitch, where she purchased a good home, with a large lot and some land. With nine living children (two had been killed at the time of the storm), she wanted to be near schools and Church activities. Polly and Lavina took their part in cattle, teams, and wagons, and moved into New Mexico, where many Church members from southern Utah had gone. Rachel and Emma would remain near wherever their husband had his head-quarters. For a time this would be Skutumpah, as this high-plateau region was called. Emma would have to set up housekeeping in a new area.

The same day Lee finished making these property arrangements for his five wives, he had a private interview with Jacob Hamblin. Lee was told that he might make his way via Hogan Wells and join a company who were making a road to the crossing of the Colorado River. Hamblin said: "There is a good place for a settlement and you are invited to take it up and occupy it with as many good ranches as you can secure. So if you have a woman with faith enough to go with you, take her along . . ." All this appealed to Lee, who grew more enthusiastic as Hamblin continued that there was feed enough to keep 200 head of cattle and that he would bring any of Lee's family or effects to him when necessary and would supply him with seeds and fruit trees.

With all this promise, John D. set about to move Emma. They had trouble enough on the road, though men had been working on it for some time. One wagon was tipped over, the stove and some of the chairs broken. They finally made camp after dark, so Emma had little conception of where they were.

PLATE I. *Lee's Ferry, on the Colorado River, looking upstream. The x marks one end of Lee's ferry cable. It was here in 1872 that Emma Lee helped John D. Lee establish the ferry service that would be the only crossing into Arizona for Mormon colonists until 1928. (Courtesy of Utah State Historical Society, Salt Lake City)*

PLATE II. *Lonely Dell, where Emma and John lived until he was taken into custody late in 1874. Emma continued to live here and operate the ferry until 1879. (Courtesy of Utah State Historical Society, Salt Lake City)*

PLATE III. *Thirty miles from Emma's Lonely Dell, John established Rachel at the Pools. In this photograph, John D., William (Billy), Rachel, and Amorah stand before the willow shanty that they later replaced with a stone house. (Courtesy of Utah State Historical Society, Salt Lake City)*

The text on the monument reads:

LEE'S FERRY
NORTHERN GATEWAY TO ARIZONA
FOR 54 YEARS—FROM 1873 TO
1927—IS LOCATED SIX MILES
UPSTREAM FROM THIS BRIDGE.

THIS MONUMENT ERECTED
TO THE FOUNDER
JOHN DOYLE LEE
WHO, WITH SUPERHUMAN EFFORT
AND IN THE FACE OF ALMOST
INSURMOUNTABLE OBSTACLES,
MAINTAINED THIS FERRY
WHICH MADE POSSIBLE THE
COLONIZATION OF ARIZONA.

FRONTIERSMAN, TRAIL BLAZER,
BUILDER. A MAN OF GREAT
FAITH, SOUND JUDGMENT, AND
INDOMITABLE COURAGE.

AUTHORITY FOR ERECTION OF THIS MONUMENT
GRANTED BY THE STATE OF ARIZONA
1961

PLATE IV. *Juanita Brooks, author of* Emma Lee, The Mountain Meadows Massacre, John Doyle Lee: Zealot—Pioneer Builder—Scapegoat, *stands beside the Lee's Ferry Monument erected in 1966 by the descendants of John D. Lee. (Courtesy of Utah State Historical Society, Salt Lake City)*

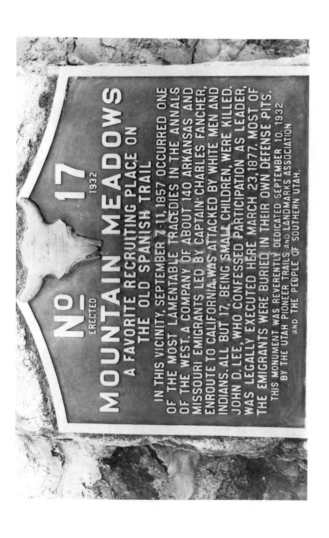

PLATE V. *The Mountain Meadows Massacre occurred four months before the marriage of Emma Batchelor to John D. Lee but its shadow touched their lives for the next twenty years. (Courtesy of Utah State Historical Society, Salt Lake City)*

PLATE VI. *Emma Batchelor Lee French (1836–1897). Her strong faith in herself and life carried her from the green of England to the harshness of a handcart journey to Zion to the opening of a frontier at Lonely Dell to her final chapter as a beloved healer in Winslow, Arizona. (Courtesy of Utah State Historical Society, Salt Lake City)*

Emma Lee

of Lonely Dell

Emma stretched her legs, turned onto her back, and looked up at the wagon cover. The three little bonnets, suspended from the bow above her, glowed in the misty light like red lanterns, symbolic of her brave front during the preparations to move again, this time to the jumping-off place of the world. As they made the descent last night after dark, she wondered if they were not literally jumping off, into what depths she could not guess.

Beside her, John D. breathed heavily. Crosswise in the upper end of the wagon, her twin daughters with little Belle between them, slept as though they rested on down under silken counterpanes. There was no sound from the other wagon, where Billy, Ike, and Jimmie were sleeping. They had pulled up alongside last night, not that boys nine and eleven were afraid, but she herself wanted them near. Eight people alone in all this big, lost country ought to stay close together.

Day was breaking, and she was tired of the hard bed and was sore from all the bouncing and jouncing of the past week. Emma was pregnant again.

"It's not that I'm getting old," she told herself. "No woman at thirty-two is really old. It's just that this young one I'm carrying is getting so heavy and active. When I try to rest, she starts to do her exercises."

Emma would slip out and look over this place that was to be her home. She dressed quietly, stepped over the end-gate, and jumped to the ground. Sand! Loose, gritty sand, piled high against the tamarack tree and around the scrubby growth. And cliffs! In the uncertain light she could not tell whether they were red or purple. Whoever dreamed that cliffs could be this color?

To the south she caught a glimpse of the Colorado River, about which she had heard so much. She had smelled it last night as they came down that last steep incline, a murky smell of arrowweeds and willows. She hesitated a moment between the river and the hill, and then chose the high road. She must get an overall view of this place.

She followed the wagon tracks through ankle-deep sand, then up a steep slope to an almost perpendicular ridge which demanded hands as well as feet, up another slope to a second ridge. She was breathing so heavily that she decided to stop; there were at least two other ridges higher up, she remembered.

The dawn was clear about her when she turned to look back—the east pink, with a thin piping of gold edging the mountain. So this was it! The sandy floor was spotted with desert brush, and there was a thin line of yellow-green where bare willows marked the course of the Paria Creek against the eastern bluff. A long isosceles triangle of cliffs was formed by the river with its stone buttress forming the base and two long bluffs coming together far, far to the north—barren it was as the second day of Creation, yet it seemed that God had tried to make up in color what He had left out in vegetation.

Over it all was silence so heavy that it filled all the valley and rolled in tidal waves to break against her ears. Distance and rocks and emptiness and silence! She must not think of the home she had left. She must not! All the things she had put into that home—the doilies and samplers, the wool flowers under a glass dome, the spray of hair flowers in the picture frame, the furniture. Then there was her garden, the arbor with its heavy bunches of grapes, the flowers that always won prizes at the fair. She had a green thumb, the neighbors said. But what could she do here?

She heard John call her name and saw him beside the wagon. How the sound carried! It was as if the very atmosphere, accustomed to æons of silence, picked the words and tossed them to her clear and perfect.

"I had to look around a bit," she answered, hardly raising her voice. "Come on up."

She watched his long strides, and as always her heart swelled with love of him. No matter what people said of John D. Lee, he was her husband and a man to be respected as well as loved. "Yawgatts" or "a man with a tender heart," the Indians called him.

As for the stories that he was responsible for the cruel, wicked massacre at the Mountain Meadows, to her they were dirty lies. Others only shifted to his shoulders a burden they should have borne themselves. Yet she knew well that was why they were here. John D. might call it a mission to put a ferry across the Colorado, but she knew it was a place to hide from the officers.

He was breathless when he reached her side. As he turned to look back, he put his arm around her and waited.

"Oh, what a lonely dell!" she cried.

"You could always make any place a home, Emma," he said softly. "It's a gift you have. We have started from scratch before and built fine places."

"But not a place like this, John. Never before in a place like this!"

"That's right. But every place has its drawbacks. In Harmony, now—"

"I'll never go back there," she cut in. "When I left England, I knew I'd never go back. Nor will I from here. When I leave this place, it will be to go on somewhere out across the river. God grant it's more inviting than this."

"Listen, girl, just before I got up, I was dreaming of the City. Then I remembered a certain day when I was invited to eat at Brother Rollins's. I met a beautiful English girl there, and later when I took her for a ride, she told me that . . ."

"You would bring that up."

"Well, it's about the same time of the year. Sort of an anniversary, don't you think?"

"I can't think of anything but this. You know it's still true, John. I did love you the minute I laid my eyes on you. And I always will. I'm just overwhelmed by this . . ."

"This Lonely Dell. You've named it, Emma. But don't you think we should go down and get breakfast? There's a lot to do today."

There was always plenty to do. For all the hard work, Emma's memory of the next few days was a lighted candle in darker hours. The air was so mild, the winter sunshine like honey, the business of setting up the temporary home an adventure for them all. First, the one wagon was unloaded and the box set off the wheels onto corner stones to keep it out of the sand. This was to be her bedroom and the general storeroom for their most precious items. The rag carpet from the living room back home was spread over the top of the regular wagon cover for extra warmth; a blanket was hung over the front entrance, a braided rug was placed on the floor. The trunk of clothing, the box of baby things, the few books, the little tin box of medicine and mementos all found a place in this bedroom. The children would all sleep in the other wagon.

There was a double advantage in having her place here upon the ground: she could get into and out of it easier, and the running gears of the wagon were then free to be used to haul driftwood logs from the riverbank or willows from the creek.

The kitchen was only a windbreak, with a tarp pulled tightly around three posts and a place for a fire in the open end. One shelf nailed between two of the posts held the supplies for cooking. With only four days before Christmas, Emma must have been busy indeed.

Christmas Eve was a clear quiet night with the stars hanging low, one luminous one in the western sky bright as if it hung over the Manger. Without any of the trappings of Christmas, they observed it, the children joining in the carols and John D. reading the matchless story from Luke almost from memory. The gifts? They would wait until the next morning—rag dolls and a double slate with two slate pencils for the twins, a larger doll that Aunt Rachel had put in for Belle (it had belonged to Amorah when she was a little girl, but it had been cleaned up like new), a pocketknife for each of the older boys, Billy and Ike, and a toy flute for Jimmie. For John, Emma had knitted a wool muffler of fine gray yarn. For goodies, she had cookies and some hardtack candy from a can hidden in the flour bin and a half-dozen apples from the bottom of the trunk. It pleased her to have been able to keep everything a surprise, even from her husband. Now it was her turn to be surprised, for she had no idea there was a gift for her.

Billy and Ike came carrying it through the brush—a chair made of willows. Arched, curving willows formed the back and arms; smoothed off willows close together made the seat. It was a sturdy chair with a beauty all its own.

"And here I thought you were chopping willows to make a coop for the hens," she said, kissing each lad in turn.

"We were, but we picked the longest and smoothest for this. Father really made it; we only furnished the willows."

"And we held the nails and hammer, and kept out of the way while he worked," little Jimmie explained.

It was all too good to last, the weather especially. She knew it, but she was totally unprepared for what happened. Just after sundown a sudden gust picked up a tin plate and sent it whirling through the air. Instantly, a regular tornado was upon them, and seemingly it was as if all the earth were moving. Scurry as they would to get to shelter, to cover things, to put anything away, there was no time. They could only huddle together in the one wagon on the ground and try to keep the cover on.

Then without announcement came the rain, a perfect deluge. At least it settled the dust, they told each other, but it also soaked all the bedding in the other wagon and most of that where they were. It seemed that the elements had all conspired to drive them from this place where no man had ventured to stay before.

But the storm did finally blow itself out, and morning dawned on a clean world. Nearly everything was found; bedding was dried; the kitchen shelter was replaced, the first flush of mud in the creek passed after a few hours. But that very day marked the arrival of the other two wagons, with Aunt Rachel along to stay until after the birth of Emma's baby and with four strapping young men to help put up a house.

Because of the storm, they decided to move farther up the valley to a cove near the west bluff. All hands worked hard, and in three weeks two rock rooms were up and covered. Placed in an L-shape design with the openings to the inside and the backs to the south and east, the rooms each had a fireplace, a flagstone floor, and a slant roof made of poles, willows, and wiregrass from the creek. They were covered with sand. Before another season they might be able to get shingle roofs, but now, in early January, it was important to be able to get inside when cold weather came. Compared to what she had left, the rooms were primitive, but Emma had not a word of complaint. Just give her time, and she'd have things nice here, too.

It was clear that Emma's time to deliver her baby had come at last, and John was away. Rachel, noting the symptoms, began to busy herself with preparations. While there had never been any sharpness between these two wives, neither had there been any genuine friendliness, for Rachel had always turned to Aggatha. Emma, on the other hand, had had a warm kinship with young Mary Ann Williams (so in love with her husband's oldest son, Alma) and later with the beautiful young Ann Gordge.

Thinking it would take Emma's mind off the pain, Rachel now encouraged her to talk about herself and her past.

"I knew in a general way that you came from England and that you were in the handcart company, and that's about all. Why don't you tell me a little about it?" Rachel said.

"Because I want to forget about it," Emma said almost sharply. "I get so angry when I even think of that song we sang so heartily in England before ever we saw a handcart, I can hardly stand to hear it sung.

> For some must push and some must pull
> As we go marching up the hill
> So merrily on our way we go
> Until we reach the Valley,O.

"Brother Brigham should have pulled one of those carts himself for just one week, and he'd never set people dragging them across the continent. Even those that went in the first companies in good weather lost too many—just plain killed with the strain of it. And almost none had provisions enough. And no one *ever* went "MERRILY" up the hill; they strained with all their might to get up.

"I have only myself to blame that I came with the late company, and insisted on coming. Brother Savage told us how it would be exactly.

He warned us. I was one that called out loudest, 'ON TO ZION.' But I paid for it plenty hard.

"I can hardly stand to go to a July 24 celebration. To this day, that song makes me positively sick. Then there are the horrors of the last camp there in the mountains, with death and starvation and freezing on every hand! Not half of that can ever be told—no, not even a thousandth part. Then when I did get into Zion, they sent me to a place where the wife enjoyed poor health. And I mean she enjoyed it! She could sit in her wrapping gown and follow me with her eyes and criticize everything I did. And the husband was always trying to maul and claw at me. I loathed him. So I left, and he complained to the Bishop. But I stood my ground. I told the Bishop I would work and earn my keep, but I would not do it in that house. So they transferred me to Brother Rollins's place. And that's how I met John. And before I had ever said one word to him, I knew he was for me."

By this time her labor was on, and she could say no more.

At last the child was born, a lovely little girl, well formed and healthy, and Emma dropped into a sleep of exhaustion. Now that they didn't really need him, John D. arrived. As she heard his footsteps, Emma called out, "Hurry in here, John, and see what I've got. Such a bonnie lassie she is. I'd like to name her for my sister Fanny, if I could find another nice name to go with it."

"Why not call her Frances Dell, in honor of our home here in the Lonely Dell? I think that would be a beautiful name, besides being so full of meaning," John suggested. "And then—maybe call her Dellie."

So it was done. All the brothers and sisters were introduced to little Dellie and were promised that after a while—when she was a little older —everyone might take a turn holding her, for she was equally a sister to them all.

The very next morning after Lee arrived home, he was attracted by the yells of a group of Navajoes across the river. As nearly as he could count, there were fifteen or sixteen in the crowd, while he was with only two of the older boys, three women, and thirteen little children:

The spirit said help them over, so I with Samuel & James & My wife Rachel Andora commenced to cork an old flat Boat & by noon we were ready to cross. When we launched the Boat, My 2 sons, Samuel & JAs. faultered, feared to venture with such a craft. My wife Rachel Andora Said that She would go over with Me & Steer. When we reached the opposite side, the Natives Met us with open arms of Friendship. They were heavy loaded with Blankets full of cloth, calico, Domestics, Made up clothing, linseys & handkerchiefs. After Much difficulty we Succeeded in getting them & their lugage over safe. Next was their Horses which we failed to swim over after 2 trials & nearly upsetting the Boat. A council was then held & 6 of their no. was to cross back & take the Horses & cross at the Ute crossing & the remaning 9 were to go the Trail on foot by way up of the Pahariere setlement. When we recrossed the 6, Night fall closed the scene. For the last 3 hours I worked through fever & ague & when I reached the fire on shore I was so near exhausted that I Stagered. One of the Natives caught me in his arms & an other threw his Blankets over Me & four of them helped me home.

The next day Lee traded them two horses and a mule for the value of about six blankets each in clothes, calicoes, and blankets. Later he traded the chief's son a fine young horse for a suit of broadcloth (evidently material for a suit), a blanket, fall cloth for pants and eight yards of calico. As a parting gift, Lee gave them about fifty pounds of beefsteak.

Through most of the month of February he and his sons worked to put a dam in the Paria and to get the water out on the land, much of which was cleared enough to plant fruit trees and vines, with a generous area worked into shape for a vegetable garden. On February 22 he started by trail with a packhorse to the settlement on the upper Paria. Here he traded items secured from the Indians for grape roots, shrubs, and seeds.

By early March he had sown a large patch of lucerne and had planted a garden of radishes, onions, parsnips, lettuce, "Rhewbarb," etc.

Now that things looked good here at the ferry, John D., Rachel, and the boys must leave. There was much to do at the new "ranch," and a messenger had brought word that Lee should prove up on the water at Rock House Valley and also at Jacob's Pools.

What about Little Belle? Would she like to go with Aunt Rachel and be her little girl? Aunt Emma already had three little girls, while

Aunt Rachel had only Amorah, who would be so glad to have a little sister. So it was arranged, and Little Belle went to live with Aunt Rachel. Belle would remain a member of that family until her marriage.

With John away to take Rachel back and things in general doing well, Emma came back again to the mystery of Ann's refusal to come out with the boys. So after the other children were asleep one evening she said to Bill, "I feel responsible for whatever happened at Harmony that made Ann refuse to come. I should never have left until the whole train was in motion. But I'm like that—too impatient, too quick to do or say things. I thought that the sooner we could get moving, the better, and so far as I knew, we were ready.

"Then at the noon camp, I should have learned the facts, instead of taking the story that Ann just changed her mind. I knew that she had no man interested in her; she had no reason to refuse to come. And you all stayed with the story that she just changed her mind."

So Bill related the story in detail.

"If they had told me that in the first place—at noon when we camped—I just might have done something about it. I can't tell now, but I just might have gone back on horseback and had Brother Redd bring her and the baby out in his little buggy to catch up with us that night. We hadn't gone more than ten miles, and I'm sure that after she cooled off and thought about it, she'd have come. I could have taken her with me in my wagon, or she could have gone with another of the teamsters. We could have done *SOMETHING*. But we missed our chance; and as Lady MacBeth said, 'What's done is done. It cannot be undone.' "

Emma paused, trying to think it through, then repeated the old proverb:

> For every evil under the sun
> There is a remedy, or there is none
> If there be one, try to find it,
> If there be none, never mind it.

In this case there seemed nothing to do but go ahead saying nothing, leaving Ann out of all conversation as if she were dead and doing as well by her little children as they could. Thus Lee himself probably never heard the full story of Ann's estrangement.

In a few days, they had all gone back, and Emma was alone with her children. She had known that sooner or later she must face this, the emptiness and loneliness. In vain she counted the improvements they had made—the houses, the stone corral, the willow chicken coop, the trees and vines set out in the clearing, the rows of vegetables just beginning to show through. She knew Rachel could stay only a few days after the baby was born, and the boys all had their work in other places. Even John had to go to the settlements for supplies and equipment, a trip that would take at least two weeks.

The Navajoes count time by tying a knot in a buckskin string each day at sunset. For Emma the days seemed like this—a row of identical knots of a dun-colored string of monotony. Meals, chores, garden, washing, mending stretched in an endless routine before her until at times she reminded herself of the old horse that pulled the sweep of the molasses mill round and round and round without ever arriving anywhere. Most of all she missed the association of other women. But the demands of each day used all her energy, and so she settled into the pattern.

"Oh, Ma, come quick and see! A big flood in the creek! It's taking out the dam!" Billy called as he came running in.

A flood? How could that be? For days there had not been a cloud in the sky. Somewhere high in the slick-rock country there had been a cloudburst. There every drop hit and bounced and gathered momentum as it ran, to arrive here thick with mud.

She could only stand helplessly by while the dam melted into the stream, leaving a gorge which she estimated to be fifty feet wide and eight feet deep. Now what of the trees and vines? How could she possibly save them? All day she pondered that problem, but by late afternoon had determined not to give up without a struggle.

They organized for action. While little Dellie slept on a blanket, the others formed a water brigade—Billy used the open five-gallon can with the willow stick handle and a nail-hole leak near the bottom, Ike carried the large milk bucket, Annie had the little brass bucket and Emmie the wide-mouthed Indian jug with its band and handle of woven buckskin. Jimmie just played in the sand. The time would come, soon enough, when he must help. Emma found a place downstream where she could reach the water, made herself a secure footing with rocks, scooped out a hole with the hoe, and dipped for them all.

Each child was to make twenty trips. Each little tree was encircled by a hollow so that every drop of water would soak into its roots. They would make it a way to study arithmetic, to find when they were one-fifth done, one-half, three-fourths, and so on. They could figure the total number of gallons and the proportion carried by each child. Tomorrow they would check to see if the trees were going to live, and perhaps would decide which ones to abandon if the task of keeping them alive became too great.

So it was that each afternoon at sunset the business began and lasted through the long twilight. The older boys took on fifty trips each, and Emma herself carried two buckets at a time while the twins and Jimmie sat by the baby. Each night, tired out, they asked God's help and direction. And finally it came, a gentle, all-night shower that revived everything and saved the vegetables. Finally John D. returned and replaced the dam.

So it was always. They were at hand's grips with elements that seemed determined to drive them out. Man had never lived there: he should not do so now. Yet somehow, just when things seemed most hopeless, the way opened up. In April following, when their supplies were low, a group of prospectors came and camped not far away. The prospectors were glad to trade groceries for baked bread, for butter and milk, and on their return left many useful items.

The World Comes to the Ferry

It seemed that people from all points were coming out to this Lonely Dell outpost. By April 5, 1872, two companies of miners arrived. The flour and the groceries they brought were certainly a godsend, and Emma soon had a splendid dinner ready. The miners remained three days and went on to their prospecting, leaving the Lee family at Lonely Dell much better off for their visit.

On April 22 another company returned, having found no gold. Emma introduced her husband to a Kentuckian who had lived in Lee's early neighborhood, and they struck up an interesting conversation. Before long several in the company had volunteered to help repair the dam, glad for the exercise and fellowship and meal which followed.

Rachel arrived also, with a load of flour and meal, young fruit trees and grape cuttings, garden seeds, and breadstuff, which she had brought as "unboalted flour." One man by the name of Rusk, supposed to be a "hard case" became so interested and happy to meet a man from his home area that he left Lee a large photograph of himself for a keepsake.

Last to come was a company of twelve men, called by Lee "hard cases." Among them was a shoemaker who, seeing a side of leather in the Lee shop, offered to put new soles on Emma's shoes if she would let him have enough leather to sole his own. Emma consented; he did a good neat job on her shoes but did not return the leather. Lee, hoping to win their good will, went out and stood outside their tent to get the tenor of their talk, and then he went in. To be sociable, he consented to play a hand of cards with them, and in the conversation he mentioned that the shoemaker had certainly gone beyond his bounds when he used up almost a full side of leather. However since the arrangement had been made between the shoemaker and his wife, Lee would let them settle it by themselves.

Emma was annoyed that her husband had not taken a bold stand and demanded that every man who had used her leather pay for it. After all, it was difficult enough to get leather out here; they all knew that. She would go herself without saying a word to John.

Early the next morning she appeared at the camp carrying the side of leather with the whole heart cut out of it. A tall, dark man at once greeted her, saying, "Mrs. Lee, let me help you with this. These fellows must not get away with this. It's highway robbery."

Taking the leather from her hand, he held it up and called out in a loud voice, "Okay! Okay! Attention all! You will every one come past this table and hold up your shoes for inspection. Every one that has a new leather sole will put a quarter into this plate. Two soles, fifty cents, and cheap at that! If the shoemaker worked free, that's okay!"

"It's no more than right!" one man called out, and leading the procession, he showed the bottom of his feet. He did not have new soles, but he had started the game. Emma went back paid in full.

By May Emma thought summer had come. Now, after having been tried so sorely by cold weather, she came to know what it was like to be tried by the heat. She was thankful for the thick rock walls and flagstone floors of her two rooms, but the spacious cellar back in the hill rocked-up in front, maintained a constant delicious coolness. Like the desert animals, the family learned to do their chores early in the morning and late in the afternoon twilight. She came to believe the folklore stories of lizards flipping over on their backs and blowing their toes to cool them as they scurried from one bush to another. Bill and Ike each carried a piece of board to throw down and stand on if they wanted to rest or stop for any other reason.

On May 17, 1872, Lee left to meet Rachel and her children who were at the Pools, where he expected to set up headquarters for a cattle ranch. He had already filed claims on the spring at House Rock and Soap Creek as he had been advised to do. But the Pools was much larger than any of these others, and located in a sheltered cove surrounded by miles of fine grazing land. Jacob Hamblin's exploring group several years earlier had discovered this spring, which they named "Jacob's Pools." To the Lee family it was now "Doyle's Retreat" or simply the Pools.

Rachel and the family arrived on schedule, and the work began in earnest. First they must have a corral in which to keep the cows, with an adjoining pen for the calves. They also put up a cheese press, for they must conserve all the milk of the herd, over that which the calves needed.

But they also required shelter for themselves; the sun was burning hot.

> Monday May 27, 1872. We commenced building a Shelter to shield us from the burning Elements of the Sun, Rachel Andora & Amorah & I pining and setting the Posts ready to receive the willows, while James & the little Boys were cutting & hauling the willows, & my Daughter Amorah weaving the willows in to form the sides.

Before they had it finished, they were visited by Professor Beaman, who had been the photographer for the first Powell Company on the river. He wrote an article and published pictures of the half-finished "shanty" as though it were a permanent home, when actually it was intended for a milk cellar. Lined with Navajo blankets, it was only fifteen by twenty feet. Later that year, Lee would start a stone house near the springs which was much larger, with cellars, two parlors, two bedrooms, and a kitchen. But, of course, Beaman's picture became the accepted one of Lee's "home" at the Pools.

At Lonely Dell, Lee also had plenty to do. He traveled there and arrived on July 3, 1872. He found also Mr. John H. Beadle, special correspondent to the Cincinnati *Commercial*. Folklore says that both men were passing by assumed names: Beadle as John Hansen and Lee as Major Doyle. Each man had reason to hate the other, but since neither suspected the other, their conversation was pleasant and cordial.

On July 24 Lee was still at the Dell, so he invited the members of the Powell party to dinner in celebration. Neither Major Powell nor his wife accepted the invitation, but all the others did. We do not know Emma's menu, but we can be sure that it was fitting, the food delicious. Walter Clement Powell wrote that dinner was good and that the "old gent" regaled us with "sermons, jokes, and cards."

James Fennemore, Powell's photographer, had been ill so much of the way that his companions feared he had consumption so he remained at Lonely Dell under Emma's excellent care. Ironically, it was he who later took all the pictures at Lee's execution.

For John D. Lee, the happiest event was to have the Major accept LONELY DELL as the official name of this place and put it on the map.

Though Major Powell had not come to Lee's home for dinner on July 24 he found it to his advantage to accept an invitation on August 14. "After a short visit the Maj. returned with me to My residence while Professor Demott, Thompson & Lady, with the crew took a ride on the Colerado in the Boats of the expedition before supper & C. The Maj. and I selected some wattermellons & got up a supper of vegitables, as it was the first in the season . . . ."

The whole company traveled with Lee to his house at the Pools, where, although it was not entirely finished, would be a home to be proud of when it did get done. They reported that Emma had got up breakfast for them all the day before, and a very good one it was, too. Upon leaving, the Major left her 150 pounds of flour and some groceries. The Powell group were all grateful to the Lee families in both homes for the hospitality extended.

Lee traveled through the settlement from August 19 to October 5, during which time he visited in southern Utah as far north as Parowan, back, and out to Panguitch, taking time to call upon neighbors and friends wherever he went.

On October 10, 1872, he arrived at Lonely Dell loaded with supplies, provisions, groceries, and clothing, about $300.00 worth. During the six weeks of his absence, a flood had again broken through the dam, and the corn was ruined by the drought. He could only cut the stalks for fodder.

During the week that John D. spent with Emma, he was involved with the Powell group. According to him, they "stayed 4 days & we built a Skift & Set them over on the 4 day. I traded to Powel a Black Mare & colt for a Henry rifle, colts Revolver & $35 cash, also let Hamblin have 50 lbs. cotton at 50 cts."

For the next month, Lee bent all his energies to finishing the large stone house at the Pools, and indeed he did accomplish a great deal, covering three rooms, putting in doors, windows, and temporary cupboards. Then came bad news: a storm was gathering, and Lee received word from Brigham Young via Jacob Hamblin that a ferryboat must be built and a road laid out on both sides of the river. Lee lost no time. Leaving his house in its unfinished state, he butchered a beef and hurried to Lonely Dell to set preparations in motion.

On New Year's Day 1873, Lee wrote, "To day we Made, or rather Emma Made, a Dinner & had all the connections togeather and enjoyed ourselves...." For ten days all would labor to build and "pitch" a boat, in addition to the small one which they had been using. Lee was justly proud of their work:

> Sat., Jany. 11th, 1873. (Lonely Dell) Arazona. About 12 noon we had a Public Dinner on the Bottom of the Ferry Boat, Just having finished Pitching her preparatory to launching her. Those presa[n]t & assisted were My self & wife Emma & her children, 7 in No. . . . Making in all 22 Persons. After Dinner we launched the Boat & called her the

Colerado & the skiff we named Pahreah. The Colerado is 26 by 8½
feet, strong A Staunch craft & well constructed & a light Runner. The
party presant all crossed on her to Christen her & take a Pleasure Ride.
We crossed over & back twice. Uncle Tommy Smith & son Robt.
Rowed her over and I steered. Set down a good Post & fastened her
with a cable chain & reached home about Dusk. . . .

Sunday evening was spent in social chatting and singing, with
Emma again responsible for refreshments.

On January 19 three of Lee's sons with their families arrived to help
their father build a home, improve his property, or in any other way
help make his living quarters more in keeping with his former homes.
They then left Lonely Dell to go back and help with the house at the
Pools—the place which had been planned to be similar to Lee's best
homes at Harmony. They remained a few days, but could do little to
change the already established pattern because existence in this difficult
terrain was so different. After a few days, they returned, happy that
they could visit their father but convinced they could do very little
to help him.

The appearance on February 1 of the Arizona Exploring Company
looking for travel routes to Arizona and Old Mexico made Emma feel
that soon Lonely Dell would be on a major travelway, which meant that
every outfit would have to be ferried across the Colorado River at
this point. The company consisted of Lorenzo W. Roundy, Jehiel
McConnell, Jacob Hamblin, Mosiah Hancock, Ira Hatch, Gideon
Murdock, Andrew Gibbons, Isaac Riddle, William Flake, Heber Mul-
liner, Barney Greenwood, Brigham Thompson, and Levi Smithson, all
of Hamblin's company, and To-ka-tann, an Indian, and James Jackson,
who were traveling independently. Lee invited six of the brethren with
whom he was best acquainted to have supper and spend the evening
with his family. They had singing, speaking, and storytelling until
almost two o'clock in the morning. For Emma, this was truly "the Bread
of Life," a sort of communion to brighten some of her lonely hours.

Through the spring months of 1873 Lee tried to manage both the
home at Lonely Dell and the Pools—the two places a long day's travel
apart. Determined as he was to get the rock "mansion" at Jacob's
Pools shingled, it seemed almost impossible. He could find no lumber

suitable, or not enough at a time. He finished up the chimneys and the gables; he set a very nice stone step; he built a mantel over one fireplace, and put in shelves. He shingled all the south side of the roof on February 15; this used all his shingles. On February 21 he wrote, "Shingling of my House so far as my Shingles lasted, Not being enough to finish the large rooms."

At her home in Lonely Dell, Emma looked forward to the coming of spring. There would be more people on the road, which meant more work at the ferry. It also meant that her husband was at home for a full month, making a stone dam, planting gardens and trees, working on the road to the ferry. Better still, on April 3, 1873, Brother Brigham had sent a group of men to work on the access roads to and from the ferry. Among the group were Joseph W. Young, Bishop (Edward) Bunker, and Isaac C. Haight, with twenty-five others. The brethren took some time exploring all the possible routes, and in the end, chose Lee's.

In time, the road was finished to the landing, with a wharf, and snubbing posts to fasten the boats securely. A happy outlook, indeed! Since the boys had caught some fine fish, among them a salmon that weighed eight to ten pounds, Emma made it the occasion to serve a sumptuous meal to all who had assisted in any way. For her it was a real celebration. Whether a "real" salmon or not, it served its purpose well, indeed.

The general Mormon plan for colonizing in the Arizona area was all dependent upon this strip of road: the access road to the Colorado River, and the terrible lift out of the canyon on the other side. The road crew, with their hand tools, could make little progress. Here Lee had an opportunity to show his loyalty. He butchered a beef, and John W. Young asked to get half of it in exchange for goods or credit.

Knowing the rules of the Church, Lee answered: "You can have it on tithing, if you will accept tithing from me. If not, I will donate it to the boys who work on the road." Brother Young consented and accepted also milk, butter, and vegetables with the same reward, a certificate of donation to the Church.

On April 22, 1873, Lee made his first crossing, taking over "33 head of Horses and two waggons. . . ." The next day he finished the crossing, for which he received a total of forty-six dollars, asking seventy-five cents per horse and three dollars per wagon, luggage and men free. By exchanging meal and flour for groceries, Emma could keep a well-stocked storeroom. And the future looked bright. Opening new settlements would mean more trade.

A young man by the name of James Jones arrived with word that another large company of forty wagons would arrive in a week or so, and asked if he could work here for his board and keep until they arrived.

On May 8, 1873, Captain Horton Haight arrived with a large company. He insisted that seventy-five cents a head was far too much for the horses, so Lee dropped the price for all horses to fifty cents.

For the next three days Lee literally worked around the clock, ferrying fifteen wagons on May 9 and twelve wagons on May 10, by working far into the night. But there was time for songs! While they were gliding over the silver waters of the Colorado, the "voice of Songsters made melody" and "all felt well." Again on May 12, the hard work of crossing done, Lee and his boys had dinner with their customers and time for singing and dancing. They had a splendid time! And were glad that no accident had happened during the crossing.

But their good luck was short-lived. The next company of nineteen wagons under the leadership of Brother Henry Day was glad to exchange soap, flour, bacon, and apples for milk, eggs, butter, and cheese. But when they came May 20, the river was swollen, the water high over the access roads, both going into the stream and coming out of it. The leader complained that this company should never have been called until there were better roads than these. Lee lectured him soundly, saying that better men than he had passed over this without half as much whining. It was truly difficult and dangerous, but all were crossed without accident. This was on Monday, May 26, 1873.

By June 7, 1873, the companies that had passed into Arizona were coming back with the report that the land was a barren, sterile desert, fit for neither man nor beast. Lee had little patience with them; with faith enough, they could have kept on until they did find water.

On June 16 a heavy gale blew up, blew a large tree into the river and freeing the ferry, which drifted off. Now they were left with only the small skiff.

In Hiding

On Wednesday, June 25, 1873, a little after dark, two of the children from Rachel's home came to say that messengers from Kanab had brought word that 600 soldiers and forty baggage wagons were traveling to the ferry at Lonely Dell, with orders to erect a fort and a military post. Rumor had it that they had sworn vengeance against Lee. This was hard for them all, for Lee was just getting his two places into a more civilized shape. But at this point, neither home was settled enough for the wife and children to maintain alone.

Nevertheless, Lee acted promptly. Crossing the river, he made it to Navajo Springs, eight miles south, the first night. Here he found twenty-two wagons of the brethren, returning from the Arizona Mission. He met others as he proceeded to his destination at Moenkopi, a remote spot deep in northern Arizona's Indian country. From Isaac C. Haight's company, Lee bought a wagon, a new cook stove and many supplies—tools, nails, soap, a big armchair. The covered wagon would be a storehouse for his belongings and probably a place to sleep.

Soon the last of the retreating missionaries moved out, leaving three good stoves that were too heavy to transport. Lee set to work immediately getting a garden planted; in this warm climate, corn, beans, squash, and melons would have time to mature. Lee sent letters to Rachel, Emma, and Jacob Hamblin. In them he gave careful direction to this place, Moenkopi, and a general description of the area, which had some small springs far apart that could irrigate a few acres. This was July 6, 1873.

On July 14 after dinner, Lee wrote Emma and gave her general advice and requested her to help Rachel to come to him for a little while. How Emma could assist Rachel when they lived some thirty miles apart, with her young children and responsibility for the animals and garden at the Dell, is hard to imagine.

Whether from overexertion or poor food, Lee became really quite ill, so that even to get himself a drink of water was difficult. When his wife Rachel arrived at Moenkopi on July 26, he thought it was in answer to a prayer through which a little bird carried the word to her. He had written the following verses in his diary:

Fly my Sweet Bird to my House in the Cove
& whisper this message to my loved ones at Home
Tell her to come quickly, My own Bosom Friend
For I am alone in deep anguish and Pain.

Just before pening the Same, a Bird came & lit within a few inches of
my head & appearingly tried to talk. I coaxed it with a littl bit and
then bid it go.

The story of the bird is further strengthened by a later entry:

Moencropa, Fir., Aug. 1st, 1873 AZ
    I will here Mention a Most Strange and Singular circumstance.
While reading My Journal to her on Page 30 [i.e., to Rachel A.] rela-
tive to a visit of a Bird that sat near My head & looked intensely
earnest as though it had a Message to deliver or recevee. While looking & talking to it, the thought [came] into My Mind if I could Send
a Message by that Bird to let My Family know My lonely & forlorn
condition, how glad I would be. These words came to Me & I repeated
them to the litle Messenger: Fly, haste, My Sweet Bird, to My House
in the Cove, & whisper this Message to My loved ones at home, Tell
her to come quickly. My own Bosom's Friend, for I am alone in depe
anguish & Pain, & the little Songster departed. Rachel replied that on
the Same day about noon a Bird came to the window . . . sill by them,
appearan[tly] tired & hungry; picked some Bread crums that lay
there. Rachel Said it was a messinge[r] from Me, & fed it more Bread.
It eat without fear, Sit on their hands & tried to talk. It was a Singlelar
Bird from any that had even saw before. When it had refreshed it Self,
Rachel Set it on her hand in the Door. It turned to wards her & bowed
twic[e] and took its leve direct towards My retreat. They all looked
after it till it was lost in the distance. The Same Evening My Son
Ralph got in with My letter to them by Mr. Winburn. As soon as the
Bird left, Rachel A. said to Amorah My Daughter, & to the children
that I was in distress & needed help & that she was bound to go to me
& that a Messinger would b[e] there soon, & went to Make ready for
a start & c. & by the time the letter came, she was ready. Thus was my
Prayers answered, & that, too, in a Maraculous Manner.

Lee had left home on June 25, 1873, had managed to get set up and
be joined by Rachel just a month later—July 26. In the meantime he
had kept a careful daily diary, recording the letters he received and

wrote as part of each day's activities. On July 26 he recorded: "I also receved an affectionate letter from my wife Emma B. Quite anxious for Me to return home. Nothing would give me more pleasur[e] to do So, for they are near My heart, but my health will not allow Me to do so."

During the month of August, Lee made no mention of Emma at all, though he wrote long daily entries. Always conscious of meaning in his dreams, he recorded on September 1:

> Through the night I had unpleasant drams; Either disaffection in My Family back [home?] or trouble in crossing the River. . . . However, being out of their reach, I asked the Lord to let their guardian Angel be near them over rule it for good. So I left the Event in His hands, Ever praying His Blessings uppon us all.

Managing Alone

It was now almost three months since John had left for his hiding place, and though she had written several letters, Emma was not sure that he had received them all. She had succeeded well with the stock and garden, but she was lonely and afraid of Indians. On the last day of August, a band of about ten Navajoes crossed the river and made their camp down near the corral. They acted strangely, she thought, just standing around uncertainly. Billy was frightened; he had heard talk that sounded like they were bent on mischief. And Emma herself had always had a dread of Navajoes.

Emma tried to tell herself not to be afraid, but it did no good; her fear spread to Billy and Ike. The twins were too involved in their playhouse to be concerned, and Jimmie was entertaining Dellie.

Emma fed them all a good supper, telling herself that it was easier to be brave if you were not hungry, yet try as she would, she couldn't help watching from the window. The Indians were walking about. Their campfire was not a big one, and she could not tell if there was preparation of food going on. What could she do? She had only one direction to turn.

She called all the children together for their evening prayer. Always they said an evening prayer, but this was different. She prayed earnestly for guidance, for inspiration to know what to do. She got to her feet with her mind made up.

Instead of locking the doors, she told the children that tonight they were going to sleep up at the Indian camp. She loaded Billy and Ike with a heavy quilt each; Jimmie had the long blanket carefully and tightly rolled, the twins carried a pillow each; and she held another and led the twenty-month-old Dellie by the hand. She guided the little procession up the path and around the corral, skirting the scrub brush, to the clearing where the Indians had made their fire.

Surprised, the chief turned to meet them. Emma explained that she and her children were frightened. Wasn't the chief, Yawgatt's friend? She would make her bed here in the camp with the children.

Clearly, the chief did not expect this. After a pause, he pointed to a place in the clearing and motioned for the boys to make the bed there. They spread the quilts lengthwise together, put down the pillows, and reserved the blanket to cover them all.

Very quietly Emma placed them—Billy nearest the fire, Jimmie between him and Ike, the twins next, then she, with Dellie in her arms, tucked the end of the blanket around her.

One by one the children fell asleep until even Billy was breathing heavily. She had planned to keep a vigil all night, but it had been a strenuous day. She was getting heavy with another child, and before she knew it, she was sound asleep also. When she awakened it was daylight. She remembered where she was, listened a minute or two to the regular breathing of the children, and raised up on her elbow to look around. The Indians had gone! She stood up. Down the trail as it wound around a hill, she saw them pass single file on the way to Kanab. The chief later told Jacob Hamblin about the incident with the comment, "Yawgatt's Squaw very brave!"

Emma looked at the calendar. John had left home on June 25, and here it was October 25—over four long months since she had seen him. Though they had figured this baby might be born in early November, they were wrong. It was going to be born now—today, and no word of Jacob Hamblin, who was supposed to bring Sister Mangum from the settlement. He, too, thought it would be a November baby.

After living through five births, one of them twins, Emma knew a little of the business attending the delivery and care of a newborn infant, so with the first signs she called Billy.

"Looks like this baby I'm carrying is determined to be born today," she told him. "You'll have to stand by and help me. But the little ones must not be troubled about it. Have Ike take them down to play in the sand under the tamarack bushes by the corral. They must not be worried about what is going on here. Don't you leave; you must help me get ready. Don't get scared if I make a noise—that always goes with it. Keep the young ones well out of earshot. You stay right close— in the kitchen."

Emma made her own preparations: the folded pad on the bed pinned securely with big safety pins, the stand with the scissors, a piece of string, and a bottle of olive oil close at hand. A hot fire in the kitchen stove heated a full teakettle, and a plate of flour browned in the oven.

She remembered her past experiences: the beautiful firstborn, accidentally killed in some way just a day before he was born; the promised twins, and Little Dellie, whose birth had brought Rachel close to her for the first time. Sweet, competent Rachel! How she wished she could talk to her now between the pains. Once when John D. had prayed God to have her pains come swift and hard, she resented it, but now she understood that a quick birth might well be better for both mother and child. She prayed she wouldn't die: with all those children playing happily outside, she MUST NOT die. Neither could she take it without some groans and a scream right at the last.

"Come on in, Billy," she called after a time. "I need your help."

The baby was crying lustily, which was a great comfort. Another girl! Almost like having two pairs of twins!

With Billy's help she tied the cord and cut it; then she rubbed the little body with olive oil all over, sprinkled some of the parched flour on the navel and pinned on the "belly-band" securely. A diaper and a little gown, and the baby could be set aside for visitors—after a bit of cleaning up in the room.

Billy carried the placenta, the afterbirth, outside in a chamber pot and buried it, being careful to go in the opposite direction from the children who were totally unaware of anything going on in the house. Now Emma asked for a drink of the porridge on the back of the stove.

"This kind of labor is really hard work, and I'm tired," she said. "Don't tell the children or bring them in yet; they'll have plenty of time to see their new sister later, when they come in for dinner. I think you and Ike can manage, but give me an hour or so to rest before you tell them. Remember to write down the date in the Book: October 25, 1873.

"I've been thinking a lot about my home in Old England these last few days, of the wonderful damp fog and the green grass everywhere and of our wonderful Queen, so I have decided to name the baby Victoria for the Queen and Elizabeth for her grandmother, Elizabeth Doyle Lee."

With the help of the children, Emma did very well indeed, and Little "Vic'try," as the children called her, grew and slept and grew some more, as well as if she had been born in the world's greatest hospital attended by doctors and nurses and endless instruments.

The baby was three days old when Jacob Hamblin called in on his way to the settlements. He had promised to bring Sister Mangum down to be with Emma, but he, too, had thought the date was sometime after November 5. He was surprised to see Emma up and about her regular work.

While he admired and praised her for her courage and skill in management here alone, he dropped a remark which she considered a base insult. It was to the effect that after a man had been cut off from the Church, his wife was supposed to leave him—at least she was not to bear him any more children. Jacob was right. This *was* Church policy. Emma lost no time telling him that this was none of his business; she wouldn't trade John D. Lee's little finger for a whole regiment of men like him! "Dirty-fingered Jake" to criticize John D. Lee in her house! Certainly she didn't need any help from him! And he could leave as soon as he wanted! Which, of course, he did.

Lee arrived home in early November, reaching the ferry about noon. He was greeted with joy by the entire family; Emma, of course, was most delighted. And his pride in her was without measure: that she could carry on as she had done. "My wife Emma had a chicken cooked & an Excellent super ready," he wrote. "She had brought fourth an other Daughter, with no one to assist her but her two litle Twins, Emma & Ann Eliza, about 6 years of age...." in which statement he was wrong, but Emma did not correct him.

It did not take Lee long to realize that the immediate danger he had feared most was past, so he at once went to Paria for supplies, flour, meal, molasses, potatoes, and dried fruit, and while there had the pleasure of visiting several of his children.

He arrived at Paria on November 9 and found two letters, one from President A. F. MacDonald of St. George, which was warm and encouraging. Lee's family and friends at Paria held several parties and meetings at which he was invited to speak.

On Friday, November 14, he returned to the Dell via the trail, and the next day he started to his main ranch at the Pools. Here he found several of his best animals missing. His large Berkshire pigs were gone and the place looked like desolation.

By Tuesday, December 2, he was back with Rachel at Moenave, a spring near Moenkopi where he remained until after Christmas. On December 29 he noted that he wrote a lengthy letter to President A. F. MacDonald giving a full statement of facts as they existed. Earlier, he had also mentioned writing to MacDonald. The following fragment seems to be one of those letters.

[Letter of John D. Lee—top of page torn—no heading or date] for the want of sufficient Team to take my Effects I was compelled to leve many valuable articles among which was a Pair of large Burkshire Hogs Some 20 bushels of Seed Potatoes, besides a beautiful crop and garden—a new Plough, Tools, furniture &c to the value of $100s of dollars, 3 young cows—Such things as I was alowed to take with distributed among the wagons of the Co. with the exceptions of two of my own waggons & one of those were exposed being drawn by a team of the Co. I had corn, wheat & Beans suffucuent to have done us till another crop could have been raised the entire Co. crossed on the 16th. I ferryed till sunset & see the last waggon over before I even went to the House to take any refreshment, & crossed the entire Co. going & returning free of charge, besides my wife Emma, cooked & fed them from 1 to two meals & as fast as a mess could cross & refresh started on to the ten mile creek to feed & water—on reaching the House I found that all the waggons had gone, except Brother Blythe & all my grain gone Some 205 bushels, together with almost every article that had been distributed to be hauled, consisting of grubbing Hoes mattocks, axes, hoes Picks shovels Brass Kettles, Pails Pans Lassoe Ropes, lead lines, besides many articles too numerous to mention. Out of 60 chickens we had 13 left Our fine Bremmeners and Polands were killed & eat on the raod by the Co. (Artillery men) Bro Jno R. Young & Capt Gibbons were along the last that left—Staid till all was safe over— Capt Gibbons informed me that nearly all my 8 [?] was gone, & that Bros. Blythe and Haskal had left nearly 120 lbs of meal for Co [?] Military men. I would rather trust my Family to the mercy of the Navajoes than to [?] as to have the Protection of such Men as I have aluded too—what they would not devour their animals would—there is land and water enough at this point for several families, it would not only be company for us here, it would save the expense of Military guard

Indians cannot cross here unless we let them over the Lee Crossing— is the only place that I know of where the River can be forded. I regret to trouble you with so much of my chin music—yet my design is good, & I trust that some thing may be gleaned from these suggestions, that may be of use. Respectfully, your Humble servant

J. D. Lee

This letter evidently made an impression upon the authorities at St. George, for they answered promptly by telegram.

St. George, Jay. 28, 1874

To Jno. D. Lee, Seniour
via Kanab

Dear Sir:

Your letter to A. F. MacDonald was received by us with Much interest. We are Glad to hear you are still intersted in the advancement of our settlements. In reguard to the Boat, built by Jno. L. Blythe & Smith, our only object was to have a suitable Boat large Enough to cross with Safety & accomodate the People. As to giving any one permission to cross without paying, we have never contemplated any thing of the kind. If you will see that this Ferry is kept up, you are welcome to the use of our Boat. You should charge a suitabl[e] price for your labour. When we come along with our company, we shall expect to pay you liberally for your Servises. We shall send chains so as to secure the Boat. See that your wife Emma gets a proper title to secure the

Boat location, as probably the Ferry May be valuable Some day & a support to your Family. We & our families are all well & doeing all we can to acomplish good.

Yours Respectfully,
Brigham Young
G. A. Smith

This communication is most interesting in that it calls Lee *Seniour* instead of *Brother* and ends with *Yours Respectfully*, both of which say clearly that he is no longer a member of the Church. On the other hand, their giving his wife Emma full ownership of the ferry—the land, the boat, the whole operation—speaks well of the impression she had made on Brigham Young.

On the strength of this telegram, Lee decided to make a trip to St. George, though it must be a month delayed. At Moenave with Rachel and her children, he was bent upon getting crops in for the coming season and discussing with various parties (among them Jacob Hamblin) the feasibility of exploring the San Juan area. However, Lee decided against going to San Juan. Instead, he planned to take Emma and go to St. George for a personal meeting with Brigham Young.

At Lonely Dell there was much to be done before they could leave. In the end, Lee arranged with John Mangum to let him have the use of some twenty acres of land if he would repair the dam and keep the water in, and care for the gardens already planted. Mangum and his wife should live in the house and take care of the children, including the baby, during the time Lee would be away. On March 24, 1874, he and Emma set out on what was to be a happy trip, indeed.

They traveled via the large stone house at the Pools, met his son-in-law Lehi Smithson, and did some trading with him. By Sunday they had arrived in Johnson, where Bishop S. S. Johnson invited Lee to speak in church and would not take no for an answer.

> While Speaking, the Spirit rested upon Me & I delivered a faithful Testimony.... Many of the audience were melted down to tears. After Meeting Father Cramb, an old gentleman from Boston city, took me by the hand & said with tears in his Eyes, Bro. Lee, you are a Stranger to me, yet may god Bless you whereever your lot may be cast. You have bourn the [s]trongest testimony of the Truth ... that I have

ever heard, though I have been a Member of this church for many years . . .

The next day they stopped at Skutumpah, where his wives Polly and Lavina Young were living. His son John David and son-in-law T. Clark accompanied them to St. George and back, a volunteer mounted bodyguard.

At Pipe Springs they were met by Brother Winsor who had the long cable chain with two locks and four keys for the ferry. Bishop Winsor gave Lee the keys, saying that Brother Brigham wished them delivered as soon as possible. Here Lee met his daughter Miriam, by Mary Leah Groves; she was in charge of the telegraph office. Since they had not seen each other for more than twelve years, neither would have recognized the other.

> Sund., April 5th, 1874. We reached Washington about 1 p.m. Put up with Thos. Clark, washed & shaved, then rode on Horse back to Prest. B.Y.'s, at St. George, leveing My waggon & My wife Emma at Washington. Found Prest. Young at home, who recieved me with the kindness of a Father, introduced me to the company, & had his wives & Family come & shake hands with me; ordered My Horse put up in the Barn & fed & had Me partake of a splendid supper with him & the guest . . . After Prayer I mad[e] ready to return back to washington to read[y] to Join him in the morning and travel with them as far as [K]anarah . . .

Lee was pleased that as President Young and his carriage passed the home in Washington, he had the team slow down while he took off his hat to Emma, who waved to him from the porch.

Lee went with the company as far as Kanarraville, then as he left, waited for a last, private word from Brother Brigham—the last he would ever receive.

> Wed., April 8th, 1874. This Morning Prest. Young implicated enjoined it upon Me to See after the Ferry & not let the Boat get away, & not let it go into the hands of our Enimies, not to hire gentiles to tend it. . . . John, you Must be careful & stand to your integrity. Blessed me & drove on.

No diary has been found for the next eight months, but it would seem that Lee carried on his work at Lonely Dell and Moenave. In May he wrote to Emma at Lonely Dell telling her of sickness and family difficulties and talked about Indian relations and affairs in the Moenkopi-Tuba City areas generally. As he did so often, he called upon her for help. She was to make sure that Billy kept the water running on the land and trees and to send all the supplies her husband and Rachel needed. Also, she was to send Billy with a wagon, 1,000 grape cuttings, tea, sacks of wheat, and cloth. And, oh, medicine for Rachel, who had a terrible toothache.

Lee's letter was evidently written immediately after his return from southern Utah. It pictures vividly the stark conditions under which Rachel was living on the one hand, and on the other, the great responsibility on Emma and the teenage Billy. He had to see to the business of loading the wagon, crossing it on the ferry, and, worst of all, getting it out to the top of what had become known as "Hell's Back Bone," a test for seasoned teamsters. From there on, the road was marked but rugged.

The whole epistle is a sad commentary on the condition of a man who once could entertain the Mormon Royalty in large crowds and who now was so reduced that a paper of tea was a luxury.

We may be sure that upon the arrival of the wagon, John D. proceeded to doctor Rachel and to prepare the earth for planting the grape cuttings. He well might have kept Billy a few days to help; but whatever they did was in an effort to provide food for another season, to get fruit and grapes established with an eye to the future.

As was typical with him, Lee did what he could at Moenave and then returned to visit his family in Panguitch. Caroline was fairly well established there: John Alma and Mary Ann lived near enough to help with the major part of the farming, and the younger children all fitted into the community life in school and church activities.

But they were not careful enough. Somehow word got out that Lee was in the area. A posse dashing into town in the early morning caught him in the corral, took him prisoner, and started at once to take him to jail in Beaver. This was on November 7, 1874.

Back at Lonely Dell, when Emma finally got the news, she said little before the younger children, but she talked matters over with Billy and Ike. Everything would be changed for them all now. Everything.

But the boat was still in her name. With it, she was assured of a good income, especially after a report that the Church's colonization would send hundreds of families across the Colorado River in the next four years. Everyone must use the ferry.

Emma studied the problem of going to Beaver to visit her husband: she simply must do that. When to go? With the fall weather so unpredictable, she tended to think she should wait—but then, it just might be that this would be the very best time. She wrote a long letter suggesting that she would wait his counsel; if she followed her heart, she would set out immediately. There would be no work at the ferry and the children were old enough to take care of each other, she reasoned. But her better judgement prevailed and she waited.

It was several months before she stopped the buggy in front of the Beaver Jail. As she approached, she heard one guard say to the other, "Who is that handsome woman?"

"Oh, she's just one of John D. Lee's whores," was the answer, followed quick as a lightning flash by a blow across his face with Emma's buggy whip. Another followed, after which he dodged and ran.

Emma brought with her cookies and individual pies; she also brought new, warm socks and a neckpiece. But most of all she brought her company and some books to read.

Between her visits to John D., she called on Brother John Phillips and his wife, the mother of her own companion wife Ann Gordge. They both greeted Emma cordially, told her that Ann was working in the Salt Lake City area and had her son Albert with her.

Emma asked them to send her greeting and assure Ann that she had only kind feelings for her, would like to see her, and talk over some things with her. They had shared many experiences, most of them happy ones. Little Jimmie was doing fine, and so was Belle, who was living with Rachel—not as well, maybe, as if they were with their own mother. But that's how life was: problems were met as they came, and sometimes decisions were regretted. As for herself, she had only love for Ann and interest in her welfare.

Emma left John reluctantly. She would like to have stayed for the hearing, but the date had not been set, and she was needed at the ferry.

Lee spent almost seven months in that small jail in Beaver, having on occasional visitor with whom to sit outside and talk. When the court did open on July 23, the jury consisted of eight Mormons and four non-Mormons. The most important witness was Philip Klingonsmith, who had already given a written confession to the court in Pioche, Nevada. The burden of the massacre was more than Klingonsmith could bear, so he wrote the story as it all happened. From his testimony, it was clear that (1) Lee was not at the council meeting where the decision to attack was made so had NO part in initiating the idea; (2) after it started, Lee did all he could to stop it; (3) Lee had orders to decoy the emigrants out and disarm them from John M. Higbee, who got them from Isaac Haight, who got them from William H. Dame; (4) his own wife had taken a surviving baby girl, nursed it at the breast, and gave it to the Richard Berbecks at Cedar City, because they had no children; (5) Brigham Young knew of the massacre before they visited him at the October conference. Under rigid cross-questioning he insisted that the orders came in Higbee's hands, he assumed from Dame in Parowan; he told of their quarrel on the ground before the men, even before the dead were buried, at which time Haight had Dame completely cowed. "I didn't think there were so many of them," Dame kept saying; while Haight insisted, "What has been done here was under your orders! You must stand up to it like a man!"

Klingonsmith could not testify about Lee's activities, because Lee had been busy getting the children loaded and on their way. Lee was walking between the wagonload of children and a second wagon that carried two or three sick or wounded.

The whole hearing was a shocking recital, a traumatic experience for the crowded room of spectators. In the end, the jury could not agree. The eight Mormons all voted for acquittal; the four Gentiles for the death penalty. Since they could not reach a common ground, Lee had to be transferred to the state prison at Salt Lake City to await another trial.

In the State Prison

During his stay in the state penitentiary, Lee kept a careful diary, which gives a vivid picture of the whole situation: the primitive conditions with no running water, no toilet facilities, no privacy. He tells of the inmates, their various activities, their frictions.

The warden came to trust John D. and to give him special privileges. Lee had dreams and in one he thought he was playing cards with the warden and drew the winning hand. He considered Rachel his trump card. She arrived and eventually bargained with the warden and his young wife to serve as cook, housekeeper, and general cleaning and washerwoman in exchange for her husband's freedom to work outside around the grounds and to spend the nights with her.

Lee had already set up a school within the prison for six young Mormon men, who were totally illiterate. He built a table for them to write on and set copy for them to practice writing. He had no appropriate books but used the newspaper as a help in teaching them to read. In this way he was spending several hours each day within the prison. One day he reported to the warden that there was trouble brewing, that several of the inmates were planning a break for freedom, but he knew nothing of the course they would take.

When the breakout actually happened, the warden was not prepared for what occurred. Each man in the group went to empty the slops for the day and bring up buckets of fresh water—a routine morning and evening task—during which an armed guard at the gate and another at the bank watched them check out and back in order.

That evening each man carried a sock in his pocket. At the right moment, each loaded a rock about the size of a duck egg. Walking in quite close formation, the first man set down his bucket and, using the sock as a slingshot, struck the guard at the side of his head. By the time each man had made a blow, the guard had not a chance for life. Now the warden and his young wife really needed more experienced help and at once the Lees became "Uncle John" and "Aunt Rachel." Neither of the young people had faced death before or knew what to do.

Despite the help and advice Lee gave the young couple, they were not a substitute for his real family. He also mentioned every letter from home, often copying parts or summarizing them in his journal. Letters from Emma always tried to be cheering; but she was lonely, and managing Lonely Dell was difficult. She needed the boys and the team.

Just before Christmas, 1875, Emma wrote another letter to John in prison. She was doing fine, busy with the boys, and planned to travel to St. George in the spring for some fruit trees. John must not worry about Lonely Dell. He was to take care of himself and tell the lawyers they would get their money once they had done their work and he was free!

Emma's letters tried to be reassuring, but other news told of problems at Lonely Dell. On February 2 Lee was visited by the wife of Brother John Blythe, the man who built the large boat of which Lee had been so proud. Mrs. Blythe told Lee that Jacob Hamblin had taken the boat and used the proceeds for his own benefit, but that her husband had reported it to Brigham Young, who promptly put the boat back in Emma's hands for the benefit of the family. Since that time Gentile Judge Spicer had been at the Dell trying to lead Emma astray with his flattery but Lee wasn't to worry because President Brown had left a man at the ferry to look after Lee's interests and make sure that no person squandered the property.

On April 9, 1876, Lee recorded that he had written Emma a long, kind letter assuring her that Levi Smithson had given him a good report of her activities at the river, reminding her to be kind to the children, and requesting that she send "all the money she could."

Among the travelers who mentioned Emma's service at the ferry was Anthony W. Ivins. The company he was with, led by Daniel W. Jones, crossed October 1, 1875. They had been joined by Spicer and Jacob Hamblin, but Captain Jones would have no outsiders in his company, nor would he tolerate Saints who would hobnob and be friendly with outsiders, so these two turned back. The other members completed their assignment, finished their exploration, and returned. They reached the ferry on June 8, 1876. On that day, Ivins wrote in his diary that the group had dinner with Sister Emma Lee, who served green corn and fresh vegetables.

Just the month before, May 11, 1876, in Salt Lake City, Lee had been released on bail of $15,000 with William H. Hooper going his bond. He was to have four months of freedom and return to Beaver for the opening of the court on September 11, 1876.

He and Rachel traveled together in a small buggy, visiting the family and friends nearest as they went. Leaving Rachel with some of her children, he went alone to Caroline's home at Panguitch, where he spent some three weeks. Here he found a loyal family, but cold neighbors: no warmness in their greetings and nothing to talk about. This, he knew, was a part of the price he would continue to pay.

At Lonely Dell, Emma was warm and loving, solicitous for his welfare, and eager to make his stay pleasant. A family prayer meeting the evening before he left was most impressive to his children: "A man's honor is his most priceless possession; maintain a good name."

The second day after Lee's departure, a messenger came with a letter advising him to jump his bonds and go into Mexico; Mr. Hooper recommended it. Too late! Lee had returned by the cutoff trail road to Skutumpah, so there was no way in which the message could reach him.

It would have made no difference; Lee would have met his appointment. Upon arrival, Lee quickly sensed the difference in the manner and tone of the trial. Now the question had nothing to do with the Church or any officers in it. The question was simply, did John D. Lee commit murder at the Mountain Meadows in 1857? Everything moved smoothly, without taking any consideration of the massacre as a whole. Did anyone see John D. Lee commit murder on that September day?

There were those of his neighbors and friends who would testify that they saw him kill two people in the wagon; another testified that he saw Lee kill a young girl.

So carefully had the questions been placed, so patient and delicate had the lawyers been with the witnesses, that the combined sins of all fifty men at the massacre were laid on the shoulders of John D. Lee. By the time their arguments were finished, he had been responsible for planning and executing the murder, in defiance of his superior officers and contrary to their orders.

Through it all, Lee sat facing the court in silence. He called no witnesses; he made no defense. After an hour, the jury brought in a verdict: "Guilty of murder in the first degree."

That night he wrote a long letter to Emma at Lonely Dell, telling her of the outcome and asking for money to carry it to a higher court.

Immediately following the sentence of death, two petitions to which more than 500 persons affixed their names were circulated in southern Utah begging Governor Emery for clemency for Lee. Again Lee was promised that if he would turn state's evidence, name the names of others present and give evidence of their actions, he would be spared. This, of course, Lee would not do.

Lee did not make the confession. Instead, he started to write the story of his life, for he was given six months in which to make the confession the court demanded. He began at his birth and followed through until 1847. During the time, he also told much of his story to friendly stenographers, who quickly transcribed it. Hurt by his own betrayal, he recounted other instances of misguided justice and unjustified murder. The manuscript was given to W. W. Bishop, who published it later that year.

In the meantime, the Temple at St. George was being completed; the dedication ceremonies were to be on January 1, 1887, with Brigham Young in attendance. Some of Lee's friends, taking note of the fact, asked him if he would like to face up to Brother Brigham and tell him just what he thought.

"No," said Lee. "Brother Brigham will not outlast me sixth months. I'll settle with him on the Other Side." And Lee was right.

The official LDS Church recorder, James G. Bleak, took the proceedings in shorthand and transcribed them carefully into the record. Charles L. Walker also made a record, but he inserted a few things that Bleak omitted.

Brother Brigham was suffering from a bad case of gout; he could not walk and had difficulty standing at all. Learning this, Brother Cottam made a special chair for the occasion, a beautiful, large, high-backed chair with a footrest and strong underpinnings so that four men could carry the President from room to room. Before the ceremony started, he was carried in through the eastern doors, while the audience entered from the north. In each room a song was sung and a prayer offered, but the main ceremonies were in the large Assembly Room upstairs. Since the business of getting the President upstairs took some time and effort, the ceremonies proceeded in some of the smaller, less important areas on the lower floor without his presence. It is reported that 1,349 people were in attendance.

The dedication of the Temple would mean a great deal to Emma Lee at the ferry, for the open and militant practice of polygamy would send hundreds of couples here to get their Endowments before they began the long trek to southern Arizona and, later on, to Mexico. While they did not call it that at the time, "The Honeymoon Trail" has become a fitting label.

Emma Lee at Lonely Dell

Although John D. Lee kept a careful diary in which we learn much about his Church activities, his settlements, and his family, we also can learn about Emma Lee and her life through family stories and folklore. These stories have grown up, until some became established as true— essentially. One of the stories often told was of the hot, hot summer of 1875. Emma and her family learned to be out early in the morning at Lonely Dell to care for the animals and work in the garden. By ten or eleven o'clock the heat would be unbearable. Even in the house it was hot; but in the large cellar built back into the hill the temperature was very comfortable, especially if a bucket of water was dashed over the flagstone floor and the canvas that served as a second door. The wooden door had to be left ajar for ventilation.

The little girls were usually content to play outdoors in the damp soil around the currant bushes or grapevines; Billy and Ike didn't seem to mind being outside so much, either. But during the day, Emma had to rest on the homemade couch on a folded quilt, because she worked so vigorously early in the morning.

One afternoon in August, an old Indian was seen on the opposite bank of the river, motioning and calling for Billy to come and bring him across. Emma encouraged Billy to do it. This he did, and Queetuse, the Indian, seemed right glad to land and finally get into the friendly shade around the house, where he rested and ate fruit. The boys would always pick what melons they expected to eat during the day, bring them into the shade, and cover them with damp burlap sacks. Some peaches were ripening and the grapes were dark, while the watermelons and cantaloupes were at their best. All of these were generously offered to Queetuse, who really enjoyed himself for the whole afternoon.

By the afternoon of the second day, he wanted to be taken back, but Billy was on a project and promised to take him early the next morning. But Queetuse wouldn't wait. When Billy and Ike got up the next morning, the Indian was gone and so was the boat. The boys could see it on the other side, and both felt that they must get it back into their own hands as soon as possible. They would finish their projects first, then Billy would swim across. Emma was watching from the front yard.

Billy jumped into the stream and started, making good headway until he hit a whirlpool, which sucked him under, completely out of sight. Ike began to scream and cry; Billy's little dog, Trip, began to yowl and bark and run towards Emma. Terror-stricken, Emma started to run barefoot down the long slope of loose sand, now almost red-hot. Her feet were being blistered, so she untied her apron, rolled it into a roll, and stood on it awhile to ease the burning. Another short run and stop, and another. By this time Billy had emerged to the top of the "barrel" and shot like an arrow toward the bank. What a relief!

Emma stood on the damp sand near the water, too grateful to think much about herself, yet wondering how she could make her way back over the burning sand. She couldn't hurry; it was too uphill. Her sons couldn't carry her; she was too heavy. The horses were all in the pasture up toward the canyon. Again she turned to her apron. She would make herself some temporary "shoes." But how could she do it without ruining the apron?

Borrowing Ike's pocketknife, she carefully cut the thread at each of the side seams near the hem. Taking out the seam on each side left the center of the apron intact, with a strip and a long string on each side quite free to be wrapped around her feet. She must not ruin this, her very best apron. In the end she had a wide-enough piece for each foot, with a long string to tie it securely. She hobbled back to the house to the shelter of the cellar, the cloth shoes quite effective.

Back on the stone floor of the cellar, Emma examined her feet. Blisters had raised on the cushions of her feet and under her toes. The bottoms of her feet were red and inflamed, but she felt sure they would be all right in a day or so. Better still, she could put the apron back together again as good as new.

"Life is full of a number of things," she told the family that night. "First, I came near freezing to death, and now I am almost cooked alive. But Brother Brigham told me that I had a great mission to perform. Not just a Mission, but a Great Mission. I used to wonder, when John set them down to the meals I had prepared, if he would count those in. Brother Brigham certainly did enjoy his food.

"Now we have been set here to ferry the brethren to their various posts: I think this might be called a great mission in a way. Not one soul lost as yet!

"I'm grateful that I will be able to walk on my feet again in a day or so, which I couldn't do if I had tried to take the hot sand barefoot. I think the Dear Lord expects us to take care of ourselves the best we can; then we'll be in a position to help others."

Then they began talking about the little dog, Trip. How unusual that he should run in his distress toward Emma! He knew, of course, that he himself could do nothing in the water, and his joy at seeing his master safe was good to see. It seemed, really, as if Trip had almost human intelligence.

By the spring of 1876, it was evident that the Church leaders were taking this Arizona Mission seriously. In May, Apostle Erastus Snow, General Daniel H. Wells, L. John Nuttall, and Lorenzo Hatch, and best of all, Bishop Lorenzo W. Roundy, the Lees' friend over so many years, all came in one company, with Jacob Hamblin as guide.

The river was running high with the spring snow melting, so the regular landing was partly submerged. Nobody seemed to know exactly what did happen or just how; young Billy tried to warn them, but no one had time to listen to a boy. They loaded three wagons, some extra gear, and several men. The boat submerged, the wagons, all the other gear, and all the men were washed into the raging stream. Of them all, only Bishop Lorenzo W. Roundy was drowned.

To the Lee family, this was a terrible loss. No other one, not all the rest put together was as important to young Billy Lee. To Billy, he was a friend who would take time to talk over his problems, always encouraging, always praising him for his skills in the river. Emma also remembered this man's defense of her husband, not just once, but time and time again. In the trouble between Emma and Ann with Lawson, he sustained the women, even in their use of boiling water. In every difficulty, no matter of what nature, Roundy had sustained Lee, and here at the Dell he had been like one of the family.

At the time of the accident Billy rescued Jacob Hamblin and one other, but Roundy dropped out of sight. Billy thought he saw his arm raised out of the water just as it went over the rapids. Later, Billy said that Roundy, now as a spirit, visited him, though he did not speak.

"During that time, Roundy appeared to me. I have always believed he came to tell me where to find his body.

"My brother Ike and I were sleeping outside in a wagon bed which was sitting on two timbers. I had a dog that would not let anyone come to my bed, even Ike, until I had spoken to him, and he knew it was all right with me for them to come. He lay on the foot of the bed asleep.

"I was awakened by a groan. I looked up, and there was Roundy bending over me. I wanted Ike to see it, too, so I nudged him with my elbow and said, 'Look here, Ike.'

"I turned my glance for a second, and when I looked again, Roundy was gone. I jumped up and searched the place to see if anyone could have possibly fooled me. There was no place anyone could get out of sight, except to run around the house.

"I went around, and in the house, where my mother was sleeping. She had her hand hanging over the edge of the bed. I took hold of her hand; she awoke startled, so I was convinced that she was sound asleep and had no part in trying to scare me.

"I said to her, 'You thought it was pretty smart, trying to scare me, didn't you?'

"She said to me, 'What is the matter with you?'

"Then I told her what had happened, and she got up and we both searched the premises, and found no one. I went forth the next day with renewed hope of finding the body of my friend, but we never recovered it.

"The Colorado River never gives up its dead."

Billy always maintained that story was true. In fact, in later years his wife recalled:

"Later my husband and I had many discussions upon the subject of religion and the hereafter. He would sometimes say that he doubted that there was any hereafter. Then I would say, 'Well, what about Bishop Roundy?'

"He would always answer, 'I saw him.'

"But if he was really there, how come Trip didn't see him?"

" 'I don't know about the dog, I only know Roundy was there.' "

Doctor Grandma French

of Winslow

Emma stretched, straightened her legs to almost touch the foot of the bed, and raised her arms above her head. She had been dreaming—crazy, mixed-up dreams without sense. She had been back in Old England with her brother, Henry, and then suddenly she seemed to be in a place, new and strange, raw, desolate, with only a few scattered houses. If John D. were here, he would have figured some portent or meaning to it all. But John was gone, and she felt almost a relief that at last he was beyond the power of evil men to harass him further.

Then she remembered: today *was* an important day, May 16, 1879. Today she would sign the deed to the ferry. Brother Johnson had arrived with word that he was to take over the ferry at once. He brought some new parts and a letter to the effect that the Church would pay Emma 100 head of cattle for her loss. So, whether she wanted to or not, she must leave. That, too, would be good; her children needed companionship—schools, church, dances, picnics. They needed to associate with others their own age; they needed a new world as much as she had when she left England. Moving would be good for them, as that move had been for her, in spite of the sufferings with the handcart journey and the problems after her arrival in Zion.

At breakfast she talked it over with the children, for all must cooperate. Each must collect his own things, sort what he would take, and leave the rest in the granary bin for whoever might find and want them. Who knows, that just might be a former playmate from Utah. Bedding, clothing, dishes, books, and a few "treasures" must be kept. She herself would see to the packing and storage of the food.

Frank French had told her earlier that when she was ready to leave, he would gladly help her; in fact, he would like to go along with her. He was a prospector who at times made headquarters a mile or so above her place, had bought supplies from her, and had eaten an occasional meal with the family. She really needed his help now, and he took hold as if he were in command.

At last the loose cattle were over the river with Billy and Ike on horseback to drive them. Frank took the lead wagon, and Emma herself drove the second one. All the children walked over the long, hard pull across "Hell's Back Bone," that terrifying stretch over which it seemed that the slip of an inch would send them literally to destruction. By this time, Emma knew that Frank French was a necessity.

They camped at all the established watering spots: Navajo Springs, Bitter Spring, Limestone Tank, Willow Spring, Moenkopi, stopping to let the cattle feed and allowing the horses to rest. They arrived at the fort at Sunset on July 16, 1879, but instead of getting one hundred head of cattle from Lot Smith, she did well to get fourteen head, most grudgingly given.

This experience helped Emma decide to marry Frank French— he was honorable and honest, and he could defend her interests better than she could herself.

As they approached the new town of Snowflake, Frank suggested that they stop to learn if they could be legally married there. At this time the territory of Arizona was in the midst of marking out county boundaries, naming counties, and preparing for statehood. Judge Stinson had succeeded in getting Snowflake made temporary county seat of Apache County. County business was conducted in the large living room of the Flake home where all the legal forms and papers were kept in a rolltop desk. Performing a marriage was no simple matter for James Stinson, for he was new in the business. But it was soon done, duly witnessed by Fred Muller and S. Willis, and signed by Judge Stinson. The marriage could not be legally filed until later, at which time the date was changed from the ninth to the eighth of August, 1879. On January 22, 1880, it was formally entered in the county recorder's books.

While we have no other written account of this marriage, it is likely that Emma and Frank would have had all the family present to witness the ceremony—present in clean clothes, scrubbed and groomed, and happy at this new relationship, with kisses and handshakes all around.

How did they celebrate? With a special supper prepared and some extra goodies—probably taffy candy cooked by Emma and pulled by the children or a hot dutch-oven cake—for this was a very important date for them all.

Frank and Emma decided to stay in the neighborhood of Snow-flake, at least for this one season. The town was in the midst of a real "boom." The first dugout hovels and one-room shanties were giving way to fine, large homes with many windows and shingle roofs. In the year just passed, twenty-five such homes had been completed, together with a two-room log schoolhouse; building on all levels continued.

In a village that size, the presence of the Lee-French family could not pass unnoticed. Billy at nineteen was a grown man, strong and athletic; Ike at sixteen gave promise of being even larger than his brother. The twins, Ann and Emma, were just blooming into young womanhood at thirteen, while Jimmie was a typical twelve year old. Dellie at seven and Vicky just a year younger, were almost like twins playing together.

Neither Billy nor Ike could be spared to go to school; there was just too much to do clearing a garden spot, getting water to it, and preparing for cold weather. Nor were the girls eager to go, when their stay was not permanent. At any rate, no mention of them has been noted in the school records.

It is likely that they did make a garden and harvest a crop and that, with two wagon boxes and the skill and energy of the whole group, they would have had good temporary living quarters, for they spent almost a full year at this place.

Sometime in the spring, Lot Smith returned from the dairy and became conscious of their activities, for on June 3, 1880, he swore out a warrant of arrest on Frank French for "obstructing the irrigation water of Brigham City." The case came into court on June 8, 1880, and the all-Mormon jury fined Frank French five dollars and ordered him to remove his diversion dam. The whole proceeding was, of course, an order to move on. They were not wanted here. It was also evident that Emma must give up any idea of getting any more cattle.

Leaving on June 10, the Lee-French family arrived at the White Mountain area in midsummer, and again needed to prepare for winter.

For two years they prospered; things were working out well for them indeed. Then came the Indian uprising of 1882, which grew into such dimensions that government troops were sent in to put it down. The Lee-French family was forced to take refuge at Fort Apache, and all their improvements were burned.

Now they gathered up their remaining stock and went to Holbrook where they rented a hotel, and Emma took in boarders. She also made cakes, pies, cookies, and bread for sale at the local stores. But this did not promise any future.

Here Ike got employment with Defiance Cattle Company and set out for himself, taking his pay in livestock.

Sometime after 1882 the family moved to Hardy's Station, the terminal of the railroad that was being built. Here Emma opened a small restaurant, serving railroad workers, transients, cowboys, and other travelers. She was a skillful cook and had the knack of making food attractive as well as palatable, so she never lacked for customers. For the first time in years, the family began to thrive.

Through all the years, Emma had kept in touch with her family in England, writing annual or semiannual letters to keep them advised on her condition and to learn of theirs. When she left home, her brother, Henry, was a well-known pugilist, for a time the middleweight champion of the area; her sister was a clerk. Emma had visited with her sister Frances Gilbert in Salt Lake City, and had kept in touch by letter, learning of her homelife and the marriages of her children.

Finally a letter from Henry told of the death of her parents and of Henry's own ill health and loneliness: Emma sent money for steamboat and railroad fare from England to America. She was hardly prepared for the broken old man who got off the train attended by a niece. Emma took them both into her home, gave him a special room, and cared for him the remainder of his life. His grave marked by a headstone is in the family plot, a monument of her family loyalty and love.

According to Arizona historian, P. T. Reilly, the French family arrived in Winslow on May 10, 1887, and shortly after Frank and his sons began building the Clear Creek Dam. Evidently the whole family cooperated, and the venture was a success. Frank's eldest son was a family man and an engineer, and his youngest son married Emma's niece from England. Billy Lee and his half-brother, Jim Gribble, now almost a grown man, were also a part of it. Emma still maintained her eating house at Sunset, serving only two meals; early breakfast and evening dinner.

Emma's real service, however, was as "Doctor French," caring for expectant mothers at Winslow at what the family came to call "The Baby Farm." She had fitted up a large room with two beds, with a roll-away in the closet if it were needed. Cowboys, ranchers—expectant fathers from any group—should inform Emma some three months in advance of a coming birth, so that she would have time to make needed adjustments. As soon as it was evident that the child was due, the mother should be brought in. She might stay as long after her delivery as she wished.

Railroad men who could not bring their wives in needed to be all the more careful to keep Emma posted if it was necessary for her to travel to the expectant mother. They must also have other help in the home, so that Emma could return to her work within a few hours after the child was born—if there were no complications. There were times when an engine drawing a single car carried Emma to the place of need and returned to get her after the ordeal was over and "mother and child doing nicely," as the paper always reported.

Already known as Doctor French, she was called in other cases of sickness and accidents, and her service was such that people more and more came to her when there was trouble: fevers, boils, infections, accidents.

Things had been going well for the family when Emma faced one of the greatest sorrows of her life. Vicky, at home in Winslow, drank laudanum and died. The newspaper carried the story:

Arizona Weekly Champion, April 14, 1888.

Last Sunday morning [April 8, 1888] the people of Winslow were shocked to learn that Miss Vicky Lee, a young lady of sixteen years

[14 yrs. 5 mos.] had, on the preceding evening taken a large dose of laudanum with total effect. The affair is rendered mysterious and unaccountable from the fact that the young lady had no earthly apparant cause or reason for such a rash proceeding. She was a vivacious, hearty girl, always apparently in the highest spirits and on the evening had attended a dance, into the spirit of which she entered with the joyous zest of a light hearted, happy girl, across whose life the shadow of pain and sorrow had as yet rested lightly.

A sister of Miss Lee was the first to discover the dire action of Miss Vicky, her attention being drawn to her condition by the moans of agony which the sufferer could not suppress. This was about midnight. The sister at once summoned assistance, but the medical skill arrived too late to be of material assistance, and the girl paid the penalty of her melancholy deed without assigning any reason for her desperate action.

Mrs. French, the mother of Miss Lee, is living at Hardy Station, and did not learn of the sad occurrence until after her daughter's death. It is claimed that Miss Lee was a daughter of John D. Lee, the instigator of the Mountain Meadow Massacre.

NAU Spec. Collections
Copied by P. T. and E. M. Reilly

In one way, the newspaper account is kind in not trying to solve the mystery of the depression which would result in this way out for Vicky. Not yet fifteen years of age, she had known what it was to be socially rejected, ostracized, shunned by girls as well as boys. This "apparently in the highest spirits" bit was probably fabricated, or overstated. To the third and fourth generation, descendants of John D. Lee were rejected: refused admittance to clubs, kept out of offices, never considered on the same social level as others. Children in the lower grades could not join in the games at recess. One does not need to guess the cause of this desire to escape.

Vicky had been the prettiest, the most loved and petted and favored within the family. To be rejected by her teenage associates would be all the more difficult for her. For Emma and her family, her death was a sorrow never to be fully explained or wiped out.

That the newsman understood the basic cause of the suicide is clear in his last sentence, "It is claimed that Miss Lee was a daughter of John D. Lee, instigator of the Mountain Meadow Massacre." That was the key to it all.

Now Emma closed the little eating house, and moved into Winslow, where she could cooperate with the family in the reclamation project. Her brother needed care, her three daughters one by one married and left the home.

Ann Eliza married Barney Haley and moved to Los Angeles. Years later, Billy's wife, "Aunt Clara," visited them and reported that they had done well, indeed, with a fine home and a large family—eight boys and two girls. The father had been elected to the city council and was much respected. They had only one loss. One son was drowned, or met with foul play and was murdered, his body thrown into the water under a railroad crossing. By the time it was found, it was impossible to determine the cause of death.

Rachel Emma married Frank Cliff, and the family knew little of them except that they lived in Stockton, California.

Frances Dell married David Blair and remained in Winslow long enough to leave three little graves in the cemetery. Only one son, Rudolph, survived; his home was Las Vegas, Nevada.

First of Emma's sons to marry was Ike, who had been living all these years at Holbrook. The date of his marriage to Bertha Avid Leevan has not been found; but they had a fourteen-month-old baby girl, named for his favorite sister, Victoria, when he was shot and killed in his own home November 9, 1892.

Joseph Fish made a good summary of it in his diary:

On the 9th [November 1892] there was a man by the name of Ike Lee killed in Holbrook. He was a son of John D. Lee and was shot in his own house by a man named Wagner, the seducer of his wife. There was considerable talk in the town of lynching Wagner. The women of the place said that if the men would hang Wagner that they would hang Lee's wife. To prevent the lynching, Wagner was hurriedly taken out of town and taken to St. Johns. Wagner was later convicted and sentenced to the penitentiary for 20 years, but he was only there for a short time before he was pardoned out, as is too often the case when the term of imprisonment is for a long period, or for life.

Ike's daughter, Victoria, was married in Pueblo, Colorado, to John James McConnell. Her husband served in the First World War and was in the Army of the Occupation until 1919. Victoria was employed in the offices of the State Board of Education in Chicago. She joined her husband in the Catholic faith. They had no children, but she was interested in her Lee background, furnishing pictures from her mother's album to Maurice Kildare, who did a fictionalized biography of Emma Lee French in *Frontier Times*, July 1964.

For thirty years Billy remained single, but when he met Clara Workman, he knew that he had found what he wanted. They were married on October 6, 1890, at Georgetown, Utah, a village so short-lived that is now impossible to determine its exact location.

Clara was indeed a "helpmeet" in the finest sense of the word; she bore him four children, two sons and two daughters. While he died at Holbrook, November 20, 1920, at the age of sixty, Clara lived to attend Lee family reunions, driving her own little Ford to one at the age of ninety-six. She made it her business to keep in contact with as many of the family as she could; she wrote stories and articles dealing with the life on the frontier. She was an ardent defender of her father-in-law, and the family in general.

Emma's little adopted son, Samuel James, whose mother was Ann Gordge, was now called "Jim Gribble" by his friends; but he was more Billy's younger brother than Emma's youngest son. After Emma's marriage to Frank French, Billy and Jim became partners of a kind.

For two years, Jim lived with Billy and Clara; then he also found a mate, Mary Effie Savage. This young lady was an active Mormon, so Samuel James Lee was baptized a member of the Church. They were married in the Manti Temple, February 13, 1894. Their family consisted of seven children, three sons and four daughters. He died in Portland, Oregon, December 17, 1937, evidently on a temporary trip there. His numerous descendants are all active in the Mormon Church, though the Lee name was a decided drawback.

One example of this comes to us from the diary of Joseph Fish. His daughter, Jessie May, was widowed early with several children.

James Y. Lee, only son of John D. Lee and Polly Young Lee, also lost his wife and was left with several children. Both these young people were in their thirties when they decided to combine families. Members of the Fish family opposed the match bitterly. The father advised against it; but he acknowledged that they were both old enough to make their own decisions and upheld their right to do so though he was not happy about it. Most of the Fish relatives opposed the marriage so bitterly that they would not attend the wedding reception or have any "doings" with this new family.

Later, Joseph Fish wrote in glowing terms of his Lee son-in-law, admitting that the couple had been very successful in raising this complex family of *my* children, *your* children, and *our* children, and admitting that the Lee offspring were fully as bright as any of the others—in a few cases, he thought, they might actually be smarter.

As for Emma, she continued her work as Dr. French, but she had some time for other activities as well—family activities, birthday surprises, wedding and baby sewing, fancy decorated cakes for special occasions.

One thing she could not change: her husband's belief that somewhere in the ledges and cliffs along the Paria there were rich deposits of silver. Though he cooperated to make the reclamation project a success, he was off again for months at a time exploring.

Emma was popular with all the grandchildren. It was always a treat to have Grandma French come to visit. She knew so many songs and riddles and little fun games; she alway carried some surprises. Her store of legends was simply astounding. Even the teachers at school would invite Doctor Grandma French in to entertain the class on special occasions.

Emma never lost her zest for life nor her love of people. She was most happy when she was most busy. Perhaps she put too much vigor into her work, because she had only turned sixty-one years of age when she began to slow up perceptibly. Frank was gone, as usual. She fretted that he didn't come home. She didn't walk quite so briskly; she sat more in her rocking chair. Frank had been gone six months. She had dreams about him; she had a premonition that something was going to happen.

She sent word by friends of his to tell Frank, if anyone saw him, that his wife would be glad to have him home again.

Then finally he did come, and she was overjoyed. After an hour-long visit, she said she would cook his favorite dish. But on the way to the kitchen she stumbled and sank down, sobbing, "Oh, Frank!" as she slumped to the floor.

The word went out that she was dying, and it seemed as if the whole town of Winslow gathered. The dooryard was filled with the most prosperous citizens; in the backyard, weeping women were wringing their hands and moaning. Indian women stood in silent groups— even some of the red-light girls were represented. Everyone had a memory of help when it was needed, of kind hands that massaged away the pain, and of an understanding heart that never criticized but that always held out hope and comfort—hope for this life and comfort in the reality of life after death.

She provided food where food was needed, raiment where children were bare—clothing that was left with her for this purpose. She did not give castoffs without helping to rework and restore them until there could be pride in the wearing.

The railroad crews, getting the word, ordered the trains to pass through Winslow quietly, without bell or whistle.

As the crowd kept their vigil, they recalled Grandma French and her remarkable healing powers. One mother remembered that in Emma's work as a midwife, she never lost a mother, though there had been a stillborn child or two. Another woman swore that chronic sore eyes had always responded to Emma's treatment; carbuncles and boils seemed to clear up amazingly fast. The little case she carried had several miracle remedies, and she knew how to use them all. A young boy told how Grandma French would always come when she was called, and that was something for a woman her age.

The crowd also discussed another case which became folklore in all the area. In a drunken brawl, seemingly a free-for-all affair, two men appeared to be mortally wounded. One was shot in the lungs, the other cut to pieces with a knife. The sheriff was advised to hold the offending actors until such time as one of the two men died, so that he could charge the other with murder. The only "physician" in the neighborhood was finally sobered up enough to examine the victims.

"No use to trouble with them," he announced. "Both are fatally injured. They will expire within a few hours."

Then someone called out, "Go get Doctor French!"

When she came, Emma ordered them taken to the hospital, where she probed the bullet from the one and spent two hours sewing up the knife wounds of the other. Within two weeks both were back at the saloon sitting side by side and ordering drinks.

As the afternoon passed the crowd continued telling stories until as the sun was about to set, the minister came out onto the porch to say, "It is over. She has gone." This was followed by open weeping as the crowd began to break up to go their various ways. Emma's spirit left at four o'clock on Tuesday afternoon, November 16, 1897.

There was no mortician in this little town. The fact that it was November and that ice was available made it possible for them to wait until Thursday for the funeral. The far-flung family was notified, as far as possible. Those who could not be reached would get the full details after all was over.

She was dressed in the new dress she had recently purchased to be ready for a wedding, and the ice packs and saltpeter cloths had kept her face clear, so there could be a viewing. The service was at the home; from two to four o'clock, neighbors and friends passed in line and viewed the body; at four o'clock the services were held in the front yard, with the minister speaking from the porch beside the closed casket.

The speaker was sincere and warm in his praise of this good woman and her services in this town, and after his eulogy, he offered a prayer. Six of the family neighbors and friends carried the casket to the wagon that was waiting with the end-gate out and a wagon cover on the floor. A sheet covered the whole to shield from the dust of the dirt road. As it moved away, the people fell into their places behind it to follow it to the open grave in the cemetery. After another prayer at the graveside, four men with shovels proceeded to fill the hole, changing off with other willing hands, so that more of those she had served might in this small way pay their debt to her.

None of them, of course, knew of Emma Batchelor pulling her handcart with the extra load of a sick woman in it, carrying a young boy on her back across the streams, that he might not have his feet frozen, sharing her own ration until she had lost half her weight. They knew nothing of the problems of operating a ferry on a treacherous river that would frighten many men, of being alone weeks on end with only her children to help with gardens and chores, of moving from one house to another and making a home of each. To them, she was simply Doctor Grandma French, with healing in her hands and understanding love in her heart.

Index